"GAELIC MADE EASY"

A Guide to Gaelic for Beginners

PART 4

COMPRISING 13 LESSONS IN GAELIC
including VOCABULARY

Written and Compiled by

John M. Paterson

GAIRM PUBLICATIONS
29 Waterloo Street,
Glasgow G2 6BZ, Scotland

First Edition..........................1960
Second Edition.......................1967
Third Edition 1973
Fourth Edition 1976
Fifth Edition..........................1991
Sixth Edition.........................1995
This impression......................2003

GAELIC MADE EASY PART 4

ISBN: 0-57970-551-0 text only
   0-88432-443-5 text and cassettes
   1-57970-124-8 text and cds

This edition published by Audio Forum
One Orchard Park Road, Madison, CT 06443 U.S.A.
www.audioforum.com

Printed in the United States of America

SOUND TABLE

A as in CAT. Never as in MATE.

E as in THEY or MET. Never as in ME.

I as in MACHINE or FIT. Never as in FIRE.

O as in GO or GOT.

U as in PUT or BUT. Never as in FUEL.

AO like EH-OO said quickly or like EU in NEUVE in French.

PH as F. Compare PHOTO in English.

BH and MH as V in VAT.

CH as in LOCH.

DH and GH as GH in UG! back in the throat.

SH and TH as H in HAT.

FH is silent except in three words FHEIN (hayn) self; FHUAIR (hoo-ir) found or got and FHATHAST (ha-hast) yet, where it has the sound of H.

IS as IS in MISSION i.e. ISH; but IS meaning 'is' in English is sounded ISS as in HISS.

SI as SI in MISSION i.e. SHI.

IDH and IGH as EE.

DHI and GHI as YE.

ANN sounds both 'Ns' though it is often sounded as if A-OON.

L before A, O, U is broad like LL in CALLING or the sound of THL.

MH and BH often sounded like W in the middle of a word, though, like V would also be correct.

I and E when the second letters of a word often sound like Y: e.g. DIURA (dyoora) Jura where DI is almost a 'j' sound. CEANN (Kya-oon) head, but when an action-word is in past time this 'y' sound does not appear. LION! (lyeeon) FILL! but LION (leeon) FILLED.

Note.—We use the 'j' sound in the imitated pronunciation.

C in or at the end of a word is often sounded as CHK thus MAC as if it were MACHK, the CH sounded as in LOCH.

RT is often sounded as RST.

D and T. Get tongue well against back of upper front teeth. T is almost TH.

B and P and F. More forcibly than in English.

G well back in throat. GOT would be like UG-OT said in one syllable.

N.B.—The accent in Gaelic falls on the first syllable of the word.

IMITATED PRONUNCIATION

Sound CH as in loCH, ch as in church. O as in sO, o as in got. ich as in which; j as in jilt; ing as in sing; ay as in day but a dull sound at the end of a word; oo as in moon; eh as in eh!

Only an approximate pronunciation has been aimed at. Anything more complex or detailed would only confuse the learner.

LESSON 31

THERE are many little turns of speech that are found in both Gaelic and English. Take for instance the phrase In my presence, which is in Gaelic AN MO LATHAIR. LATHAIR (la- hir) 2. presence: also AN LATHAIR, in presence or, simply, present. Now if you remember how in the phrase THA MI AN MO SHEASAMH the AN MO was shortened to 'NAM you will not be surprised to find the same thing happening to AN MO LATHAIR which becomes 'NAM LATHAIR. Likewise 'NAD LATHAIR, in your presence and 'NA LATHAIR, in his, her or its presence. Again 'NAR LATHAIR, in our presence, 'NUR LATHAIR, in your presence and 'NAN LATHAIR, in their presence. AM MEASG In midst (of) has 'NAR MEASG, in our midst or among us and so on. MEASG (mesk) can also be used as an action-word MEASG! Mix! BHA AM FION AIR A MHEASGADH LE UISGE. The wine was mixed with water.

AN AGHAIDH (uGHy) means in face (of) or against. DH'IOMAIR IAD AN AGHAIDH AN T-SRUTHA. They rowed in face of (against) the stream. Notice, by the way, that many of these phrases are followed by the "of" form of the name-word. Thus AN SRUTH, 1. The stream. AN T-SRUTHA, Of the stream. Against me is 'NAM AGHAIDH (nam uGHy) 'NA AGHAIDH, Against him or it, 'NA H-AGHAIDH Against her or it. But notice, however, 'NAR N-AGHAIDH, Against us, and 'NUR N-AGHAIDH, Against you. CHUIR IAD 'NAR N-AGHAIDH GACH UAIR, They put against (or opposed) us every time. Note that words like AGHAIDH which begin with a vowel always take an extra N- in the "our" and "your" forms.

1

Many phrases begin with AIR, on. Thus AIR BEULAOBH, on (in) front (of) BEULAOBH (**bayl-uv**). THA REIDHLEAN AIR BEULAOBH AN TAIGHE, There is a green in front of the house. REIDHLEAN (ray-lan) 1. green, bowling-green. CHARAICH AN SGOILEAR A LEABHAR-SGRIOBHAIDH AIR BEULAOBH A' MHAIGH-STIR, The pupil laid his writing-book before the master. CAIRICH! lay! place! (**ka-reeCH**): CARADH (**ka-ruGH**) laying. LEABHAR-SGRIOBHAIDH, writing-book. AIR MO BHEUL-AOBH (**er mO vayl-uv**) before me and so on. AIR AM BEULAOBH, before them. BHA COILLE MHOR AIR AR BEULAOBH, There was a great wood before us.

FA CHOMHAIR (**fa CHo-ir**) means also before, in front of or in view of, and has the further meaning of preparing for something that is to happen. SHEAS AM PRIOSANACH FA CHOMHAIR A' BHREITH-EIMH, The prisoner stood before (opposite) the judge. RINN IAD ULLACHADH MOR FA CHOMHAIR TEACHD AN RIGH, They made great preparation for (in anticipation of) the coming of the king. ULLACHADH (**oolaCH-uGH**) 1. preparation. TEACHD (**cheCHk**) 1. arrival, coming.

FA MO CHOMHAIR, before or opposite me etc. Note FA CHOMHAIR, before him or it: FA COMHAIR (**ko-ir**) before her or it. FA'R COMHAIR, before us: FA UR COMHAIR, before you: FA' COMHAIR, before them.

MU THIMCHIOLL (**mu-hima-Chyol with stress on hima**) about, concerning. MU THIMCHIOLL FICHEAD, about twenty. FICHEAD (**feeCH-ud**) twenty. BHA E A' BRUIDHINN MU THIM-CHIOLL NAN NITHEAN SEO, He was speaking about (concerning) these things. Now just as AN MO becomes shortly 'NAM so MU MO becomes MU'M; MU DO, MU D'; etc., and so we have MU'M THIMCHIOLL, about me. MU D' THIMCHIOLL about thee (you): M'A THIMCHIOLL, about him (or it): M'A TIMCHIOLL, about her (or it): MU AR or M'AR TIMCHIOLL, about us: MU UR or M'UR

2

TIMCHIOLL, about you, and MU AN or M'AN TIMCHIOLL about them. TIMCHIOLL (**Chima-CHyol**) 1. means circuit or a going round. It can also be used thus, THA I AG OBAIR TIMCHIOLL AN TAIGHE, She is working about the house. TIMCHIOLL takes the "of" form of the name-word after it. RUITH A' CHLANN TIMCHIOLL OIRNN, The children ran round about (on) us. TIMCHIOLL AIR, round or around.

DO MO IONNSUIDH (**do mO yoonsy**) means towards (or to) me, and is also written DO M'IONNSUIDH. Likewise DO D'IONNSUIDH towards you, D'A IONNSUIDH towards him (or it): D'A H-IONNSUIDH, towards her (or it): DO AR N-IONNSUIDH, towards us: DO UR N-IONNSUIDH, towards you and DO'N IONNSUIDH, towards them. A DH'IONNSUIDH (**a yoonsy**) itself means towards, coming from DO doubled and IONNSUIDH, the two DO's being reduced to A DH'.

Faclair

CEARN (**kyarn**) 1. corner, region. SAOGHAL (**soo-GHal**) 1. world: also lifetime. LUCHAIRT (**looCH-arsht**) 2. palace. CASAID (**kas-ej**) 2. complaint also CASAID! complain! BIADH (**bee-uGH**) 1. food. AS AN AGHAIDH, to their face. AITHISG (**ah-ishk**) 2. report. FEAR-AITHISG, reporter. FEAR-EAGAIR (**fer ek-ir**) 1. editor. EAGAR, 1. order, class, arrangement. CARAICH! (**ka-reeCH**) place! also move! SLOIGH (**sloy**) 1. Crowds. NOCHD! (**noCHk**) appear! show! AN DEIDH (**un jay**) after; 'NAM DHEIDH (**nam yay**) after me; NA DEIDH after her, it. NAN DEIDH after them and so on. This is also written AS DEIDH, after; and so, AS MO DHEIDH, after me, etc. FEAR-TURUIS (**fer toorish**), tourist, traveller. TURUS (**toorus**) 1. journey. DEOCH (**joCH**) 2. drink. THUG (**hook**) brought, gave, paid. AM FALACH (**fal-aCH**) 1. in hiding, hidden. CLISGEADH (**kleesh-guGH**) 1. start. GOIRID AS (**gurij ass**), short way off. BHUAPA (**vooa-pa**) from them. SGRIOB (**skreeb**) 2.

visit ; also, Scrape! LARACH (**la-raCH**) 2. ruin, site of building. TOLMAN, 1. knoll. OS CIONN (**oss kyown**) above. OS MO CHIONN (**oss mO CHyown**) above me ; and so on. BRAS (**brass**), swift, impetuous. AIR CULAOBH (**er kooluv**) behind. AIR MO CHULAOBH (**er mO CHooluv**) behind me, etc. CUM A MACH! (**koom a maCH**) maintain! CUMAIL (**koom-il**) A MACH maintaining. NEO-CHIONTACH (**nyo Chunn-taCH**) innocent. COACHLADH (**kooCH-luGH**) 1. change. A CHAOCHLADH (**a CHooCH-luGH**) its change, reverse or opposite. FIOR (**feer**) true, just.

Gaelic to English

Cha robh moran daoine an lathair. A mach as mo lathair. Cha do thuirt (or d' thuirt) e facal 'nan lathair. Bha daoine as gach cearn de'n t-saoghal am measg an t-slaugh a chruinnich aig an luchairt. Bha meirlich 'nam measg cuideachd. Sheol am bata an aghaidh na gaoithe. Bha an sruth 'nar n-aghaidh. Rinn na gillean casaid 'na h-aghaidh air son nach robh am biadh deas. Thuirt mi as an aghaidh riu na bha 'nam bheachd. Chuireadh e 'nam aghaidh anns a h-uile rud a dheanainn. Bha craobh ard air beulaobh na sgoile. Dheasaich am fear-aithisg sgeul air a' mhort agus charaich e air a' bhord i air beulaobh an fhir-eagair. Sheas na sloigh mu thimchioll luchairt na banrigh agus nochd i tri uairean fa'n comhair. An deidh uine fhada, thug am fear-turuis a mach an tombaca agus an deoch laidir a bha aige am falach m' a thimchioll. Thug e clisgeadh as na daoine an uair a chunnaic iad an tarbh a bha goirid bhuapa a' tighinn do an ionnsuidh. Thug sinn sgriob a dh'ionnsuidh larach na seann eaglaise a bha air tolman os cionn na coille. Bha abhainn bhras air ar culaobh agus creag chas air ar beulaobh. Tha e a' cumail a mach gum bheil e neo-chiontach ach tha mi anns a' bheachd gum bheil a chaochladh fior.

Translation

There weren't many people present. Out of my presence! He did not say a word in their presence.

4

There were people from every corner of the world among the crowd that gathered at the palace. There were thieves among them also. The boat sailed against the wind. The stream was against us. The boys made a complaint against her because the food wasn't ready. I said outright to them what was in my mind. He would oppose me in everything that I would do. There was a tall tree in front of (facing) the school. The reporter got ready the report on the murder and laid it on the table before the editor. The crowds stood around the palace of the queen and she appeared three times before them. After a long time the tourist brought out the tobacco and spirits which he had concealed about him. It gave the people a start when they saw the bull, which was a short distance off, coming towards them. We paid a visit to the ruins of the old church that was on a knoll above the wood. There was a fast running river behind us and a steep rock in front of us. He maintains that he is innocent, but I am of the opinion that the reverse is true.

LESSON 32

IN this lesson we are going to see how persons and things are compared in Gaelic. Take the sentence, THA IAN CHO MOR RI TOMAS, John is as big as Thomas. We are showing that two persons are equal as regards height and the ' as . . . as ' is turned into Gaelic by CHO . . . RI.

BHA AN DUINE BOCHD CHO MARBH RI SGADAN, The poor chap was as dead as a herring.

CHAN 'EIL I CHO LAIDIR RIUT-SA, She is not as strong as you.

BHA AM FAMHAR CHO ARD RI MULLACH AN TAIGHE, The giant was as tall as the top of the house. FAMHAR (fav-ar) 1. giant. But if the second 'as' is followed by a sentence we use AGUS which also means 'as' (often shortened to 'S) instead of RI.

THA IAD A CHEART CHO CAIRDEIL AGUS ('S) A BHA IAD ROIMHE. They are just as friendly as they were before.

THIG CHO LUATH AGUS IS URRAINN DUIT. Come as soon as you can.

A CHEART (a CHyarst) just. CAIRDEIL (kar-jil) friendly.

BITHIBH CHO MATH AGUS ('S) AN T-IM A CHUR A NALL, Be as good as (or, kindly) pass over the butter. A NALL (a naool), from the side that is over, or opposite to the speaker. Note the order above, i.e. The butter to put over.

Besides being equal, persons and things may also be unequal to each other in some respect, i.e. taller, stronger or less than each other. Now the -er form of the word is got by putting an 'i' into the Gaelic word (if there isn't one there already) and adding an 'e' at the end. Thus ARD, tall or high. AIRDE (arj-a) taller or higher. BAN, fair. BAINE (ban-ya) fairer. GRINN (greeng) fine. GRINNE (greenn-ya) finer.

6

This, you will notice, is the same as the 'of' form of Class 2 name-words. Let us consider a few examples.

THA AN CNOC SEO NA'S AIRDE NA AN CNOC EILE, This hill is higher than the other hill. The NA'S AIRDE NA stands for NA IS AIRDE NA, What is higher than.

THA MAIRI NA'S BAINE NA SINE, Mary is fairer than Jean.

RUITHIDH FIADH NA'S LUAITHE NA CU, A deer will run faster than a dog. LUAITHE (looay-ha) faster.

In past time we change NA'S (NA IS) into NA BU. Remember that BU sharpens the following word if possible.

BHA MAIRI NA BU BHAINE NA SINE, Mary was fairer than Jean.

BHA E NA B'OIGE NA A BHRATHAIR, He was younger than his brother.

RUITH IAIN NA BU LUAITHE NA SEUMAS, John ran faster than James.

BHA AN T-AIRGIOD NA BU GHAINNE AN UAIR A BHA MI OG, (The) Money was scarcer (what, or something that, was scarcer) when I was young.

Very often we can use IS and BU to begin sentences such as we have above, instead of THA and BHA. For instance, THA MAIRI NA'S BAINE NA SINE might be put quite neatly IS BAINE MAIRI NA SINE, 'Tis fairer Mary than Jean. Again we might say IS I MAIRI A'S BAINE NA SINE, 'Tis she, Mary, that is fairer than Jean ; and this is making our statement a little stronger.

IS LUAITHE FIADH NA CU, A deer is faster than a dog.

BU BHAINE MAIRI NA TE EILE DE'N CHUID-EACHD, Mary was fairer than anyone else in (of) the company.

NACH E SEO AN TAOBH A'S FUAIRE DE'N TAIGH? Is not this the colder side (i.e. that is colder) of the house?

When in English we compare one object with two or more other objects we may say that it is the finest, heaviest, dearest of all. The '-est' form is the same in Gaelic as for the '-er' form, the context i.e. what comes after, telling which is meant.

IS E IAIN A'S OIGE DE'N TEAGHLACH. It is John that is youngest of the family. TEAGHLACH **(tyaoo-laCH)** 1. family. IS E AN COTA A'S DAOIRE ANNS A' BHUTH, It is the dearest coat in the shop. B'IAD SUD NA LAITHEAN A BU SHONA DE MO BHEATHA, Those (or yon) were the happiest days of my life. Note that SONA makes no change in its form, like most words ending in 'a'. IS E IAIN A'S OIGE might mean, 'Tis IAIN that is younger (of the two) or youngest, but the addition of DE'N TEAGHLACH leaves no doubt in the mind as to what is meant.

Faclair

LUAIDH **(looa-ee)** 1. or 2. lead. CURRAC **(kur-raCHk)** 1. Woman's cap. AN T-SUAIN **(an tooayn)** 2. Sweden. SMEORACH **(smyo-raCH)** 2. mavis, thrush. DOIRE **(durra)** 2. grove, oak-wood. FIONNAR **(fyoon-nar)** cool. RE **(ray)** during. SAOIL! **(sooil)** think! TUIGSEACH **(toog-shaCH)** knowing, expert. GIULLACHD **(gyool-aCHk)** 2. management. BAILE-FEARAINN **(bala fer-ing)** 1. farm, farm-town. CARAICH! **(ka-reeCH)** repair! CARADH repairing first 'a' long. TRIUIR **(troo-ir)** trio. UACHDAR **(ooaCHk-ar)** 1. surface, top. COMHNARD **(kO-nard)** level; also, a plain, CI. 1. FANN **(faoon)** weak. COSNADH **(kos-nuGH)** 1. work, employment. MI-MHODHAIL **(me-vOil)** ill-mannered.

Gaelic to English

Bha an leabhar cho trom ri cnap luaidhe. Tha currae a' bhoirionnaich sin cho geal ris an t-sneachd. Tha mo bhata-sa na's grinne na do bhata-sa. Is e mo bhata-sa a's grinne na do bhata-sa. Is grinne mo bhata-sa na do bhata-sa. Tha Alba cho beartach ris an t-Suain. Bidh Morag na's airde na a brathair. Is binne leam do ghuth na smeorach na doire. Bha e moran na b' fhionnaire anns an fheasgar na bha e re an la. Tha an te na's daoire na an t-im an drasda ach is e an cafe a's daoire

de na h-uile. Is e seo an taobh a's fuaire de'n eilean.
Saoilidh mi gur e Calum a's tuigsiche a thaobh giullachd baile-fearainn. Nach i Mairi Mhor a's oige de'n
triuir? Bha uachdar an rathaid na's comhnairde na
bha e roimhe an deidh dha a bhi air a charadh. Is trice
do'n aimsir a bhi fliuch na tioram anns an aite seo.
Bha an duine bochd a' fas na b'fhainne. Cha b'e am
biadh a bu ghainne ach an cosnadh agus an t-airgiod.
Is i a' chaileag a's mi-mhodhaile anns a' bhaile.

Translation

The book was as heavy as a lump of lead. The
head-dress of that woman is as white as (the) snow.
My boat is finer than your boat. 'Tis my boat that's
finer than your boat. 'Tis finer my boat than your
boat. Scotland is as rich as Sweden. Morag will be
taller than her brother. I think your voice sweeter
('Tis sweeter with me) than the mavis of the grove.
It was much cooler in the evening than it was during
the day. (The) Tea is dearer than (the) butter at
present but (the) coffee is dearest of all. This is the
coldest (or colder) side of the island. I am thinking
that it's Calum that's most knowledgeable with regard
to management of a farm. Isn't it Big Mary that's
the youngest of the trio? The surface of the road
was more level than it was before after it was repaired
(after to it to be). The weather is more often wet (it
is more often for the weather to be wet) than dry in
this place. The poor man was growing weaker. It
wasn't the food that was scarcest but employment and
money. She is the most ill-bred girl in the town.

LESSON 33

WE find in English that although we may say of a person that he is 'tall' and of another that he is 'taller' we cannot also say one person is 'good' and that another is 'gooder'. Rather must we use a different word namely 'better'. Similarly 'bad' or 'evil' change to 'worse': and so on for a number of other words. Something the same happens to a few words in Gaelic. Here they are:

MATH, good: FEARR (**fyarr**) better.

OLC (**olk**) evil: MIOSA (**missa**) worse. DONA, bad: DONA, worse.

BEAG, small: LUGHA (**loo-a**) smaller or less. BIGE (**beeka**) is also used.

LAIDIR (**la-jir**) strong: TREASA (**tressa**) or LAIDIRE (**la-jeer-a**) stronger.

Some appear to shorten as:

MOR, big: MO or MOTHA (**mo-a**) bigger.

GOIRID (**gur-ij**) short: GIORRA (**gyirra**) shorter.

FURASDA (**foor-as-da**) easy: FASA, easier.

DUILICH, difficult: DORRA (**dorra**) more difficult; also DUILGHE (**dool-ee-ya**).

TETH (**chay**) hot gives TEOTHA (**cho-a**) hotter.

Here are a few examples showing their use:

THA IAIN NA'S TREASA NA SEUMAS, Iain is stronger than James.

GED IS DONA MAC AN ABA, IS MIOSA A BHRATHAIR, Though MacNab is bad, his brother is worse.

IS FEARR DHUIT FALBH, You had better go: i.e. 'Tis better for you going. But IS FEARR LEAM AN DUTHAICH NA AM BAILE, I prefer the country to the town: i.e. 'Tis better with me, or, I consider (to be) better. Note this use of LE to give a person's opinion.

10

AM FEAR A'S LUGHA DE'N TRIUIR, The smallest man of the three. TRIUIR (**troo-ir**) three.

BHA RATHAD A' CHLADAICH FADA NA BU DORRA, The shore-road was far more difficult. Observe that 'was more difficult' is translated by NA BU DORRA and not by NA'S DORRA because we are speaking in past-time. CLADACH (**klad-aCH**) 1. stony shore.

The putting in of the 'I' when forming the -er and -est forms of describing-words often changes the sound and may sometimes shorten the words just as we saw happened to name-words. For example: O words change to UI. TROM, heavy becomes TRUIME (**trooim-a**) heavier, or heaviest. Thus NA'S TRUIME, heavier: A'S TRUIME, heaviest. Similarly GORM, blue, becomes GUIRME (**gooirm-a**): BOG, soft, damp, becomes BUIGE (**booee-ga**).

EA words change to EI or I as BEAG, small: BIGE (**beega**) smaller. GEAL, bright: GILE (**geela**) brighter. SEARBH, bitter: SEIRBHE (**shayruv-a**) more bitter. CINNTEACH, certain: CINNTICHE (**keenj-ee-CHa**) more certain. DEARG, red: DEIRGE (**jay-rug-a**) redder. DEAS, ready: DEISE (**jaysh-a**) readier.

IA and EU words change to EI: GEUR, sharp: GEIRE (**gayra**) sharper. DIAN (**jeean**) hasty, or violent: DEINE (**jayna**) hastier or more violent.

IO and IU words change to I. CRION (**kreen**) withered: CRINE (**kreena**) more withered. FLIUCH, wet: FLICHE (**fleeCHa**) wetter.

Some words such as SONA, happy, GASDA, fine, BLASDA, tasty, do not change. Others may shorten as BOIDHEACH, pretty: BOIDHCHE (**boee-CHa**).

THA MAIRI MORAN NA'S SONA A NIS, Mary is much happier now.

IS E AN T-AODACH SEO A'S UAINE, It is this cloth that is greenest. These -er and -est forms can be used to form many useful phrases, as:

A'CHAILEAG A'S GILE SNUADH, The girl that's fairest (as regards) complexion. The girl with the fairest complexion. SNUADH (**snoo-uGH**) 1. complexion.

AM FEAR A B'AIRDE CLIU, The man that was highest (as regards) reputation: The man with the highest reputation. CLIU (**klyoo**) 1. or 2. reputation, praise.

To say that a person is the better or worse as regards something is got by tacking -DE on to the end of FEARR, MIOSA etc. This -DE which means 'of' may cause a slight change in some words.

IS FEAIRRDE THU SIN means the same as IS FEARR THU DE SIN, you are better of or for that. Note how the -DE has put an I into FEARR. FEAIRRDE (**fyar-ja**) is often written FHEAIRRD and with IS would sound (**sharj**). After BU, was or were, we would have B'FHEAIRRD (**byarj**).

AM B'FHEAIRRD AM BALACH A GHREIDH-EADH? Was the boy the better for his thrashing? GREIDHEADH (**gray-uGH**) 1. thrashing. The object with regard to which the person is better or worse is put at the end of the phrase. The answer to the above question might be CHA B'FHEAIRRD E IDIR E, He wasn't the better of it at all, or more simply CHA B'FHEAIRRD.

AM BU MHISDE A' CHAILEAG A TUMADH? Was the girl the worse for her ducking? CHA BU MHISDE, No. It is not necessary to repeat the object in the reply. MISDE (**mis-ja**) worse of. TUM! (**toom**) immerse! TUMADH (**toom-uGH**) 1. immersion.

Here are one or two other useful phrases:

MAR IS MO, IS ANN IS FHEARR, The more the better, i.e. As 'tis more, 'tis so, 'tis better.

MAR BU SHINE A DH'FHAS E, B'ANN (or IS ANN) BU MHIOSA A BHA E A' FAS. The older he grew 't was (or 'tis) the worse he was growing.

AIR CHO FUAR 'S A BHA AN LA, CHA ROBH COTA AIR IDIR, However (or no matter how) cold the day was, he had no coat on at all.

AIR CHO TRIC 'S A DH'ITHEADH E, BHIODH AN T-ACRAS DAONNAN AIR, No matter how (or however) often he would eat he was always hungry.

AIR CHO FUAR 'S GUM BI AN LA, THIG E, No matter how cold (that) the day will be, he will come.

12

Faclair

SINE (**shina**) older. TEIRINN (**chay-ring**) descend: TEARNADH (**char-nuGH**) descending. FAIDE (**faja**) further, like FHEARR if often written FHAIDE after IS, thus IS FHAIDE (**saja**). RUISG (**rooishg**) strip peel: RUSGADH (**roosg-uGH**) peeling, stripping. GIORRAID (**gir-rij**) shorter of, or, shorter by, FEARCHAR (**fera-CHar**) Farquhar. TAPAIDH (**tap-ee**) smart. MEAS! (**mayss**) consider! esteem! calculate! MEAS or MEASADH considering etc. TRUIMID (**troorm-ij**) heavier for. FADA, long, far: FAIDE (**fa-ja**) longer, further.

Gaelic to English

Am balach a's miosa. A' chlach a's motha. An rathad a's giorra. Is truime Iain na Domhnull. Bha e na bu fhliche an diugh na bha e an de. An leasan a b'fhasa anns an leabhar. B'e Alasdair a b'oige de'n teaghlach. Is sine Mairi na Anna. B'e tearnadh a' chnuic a bu dorra. Mar is luaithe is ann is fearr (or fhearr). Cha b'urrainn daibh dol na b' fhaide. Tha seo cho geal ri sin. Tha falt an duine sin na's gile na an sneachd. Is misde a' chraobh a rusgadh. Is giorraid an rop am mir ud a bhi dheth. B' fheairrd an duine bochd an deoch ud. B' e sud am biadh a bu bhlasda a fhuair mi a riamh. B'e Caoilte an gaisgeach a bu luaithe ceum. Air cho sgith 's a bhiodh Fearchar, chuireadh e daonnan crioch air obair an la. Air cho tapaidh 's gum meas sinn Seumas, cha chreid mi gun coisinn e an duais. Cha truimid mo phoca an t-airgiod a thug am meirleach as. Mar a b'fhaide a chaidh sinn a mach is ann a b'fhuaire a bha an t-uisge.

Translation

The worst boy, or, the boy that is worse. The biggest stone, or, the bigger stone. The shortest road, or, the shorter road. Iain is heavier than Donald. It was wetter to-day than yesterday. The easiest lesson (the lesson that was easiest) in the book. Alexander was the youngest of the family. Mary is older than Ann. It was descending the hill that was the more difficult. The sooner the better. They couldn't go any further. This is as white as that. That man's hair is whiter than snow. The tree is the worse of its stripping. The rope is the shorter by that bit being off. The poor fellow was the better of that drink. That was the tastiest food I ever got. Caoilte was the hero with the quickest step. However tired Farquhar might be, he would always finish the day's work. No matter how clever we consider James, I don't believe he will gain the prize. My pocket is none the heavier for the money the thief took out. The further we went out the colder the water was.

LESSON 34

IN this lesson we are dealing with the word SEE in its different forms and just as in English we find I see, saw, have seen (changes which take place in other languages as well), so we may expect something of the same in our own. Starting from the word of command we say:

FAIC CO THA A' TIGHINN! See who is coming!

AM FAIC MI AN NOCHD THU? Shall I see you to-night?

CHAN FHAIC, ACH CHI MI AM MAIREACH THU MA BHIOS SIN FREAGARRACH. No, but I shall see you to-morrow if that will be suitable. FREAGARRACH (**frek-a-raCH**) suitable. FAIC (**feCHk**) see. CHAN FHAIC (**CHan eCHk**). CHI (**CHee**) shall or will see.

AM FAIC THU LONG NAN CRANN ARDA? Do you see the ship with the tall masts? CHI, I do. CHAN FHAIC, I don't. CRANN (**kraoon**) 1. mast.

THA E AG RADH NACH FHAIC E AN LONG. He says he doesn't see the ship.

You will notice that we did not say FAICIDH for 'shall see' but used another word CHI. CHA becomes CHAN, for having sharpened F to FH which is silent, the first letter of the second word is the vowel A.

A point to remember also is that when an action-word has two forms as for example THA (BHEIL): BHA (ROBH): CHI (FAIC): CHAIDH (DEACH-AIDH) etc., we always use the second form after AN (AM). CHA, NACH, GUN (GUM), MUR; NAN (NAM), but the first form after MA, GED, and A meaning Person or Thing that; also NA meaning What or Those that.

Now let us consider a statement in past time:

CHUNNAIC MI NA CLUICHEAN AN DIUGH, I saw the games to-day.

AM FACA UR CAIRDEAN IAD? Did your friends see them?

CHAN FHACA AGUS IS BOCHD LEAM NACH FHACA, They didn't and I think it a pity they didn't. IS BOCHD, It's a pity: IS BOCHD LEAM, I think it a pity.

FACA (faCHka) saw. NACH FHACA (naCH aCHka) didn't see. Here we have two words, CHUNNAIC (1st form) and FACA (2nd form) though CHUNNAIC is already known to you. We should not really sharpen FACA after NACH but it is usually done.

The 'should' and 'would' forms are quite simple coming as they do from CHI and FAIC. CHITHINN (CHee-ing) I should see: CHITHEAMAID (Chee-a-mij) We should see, the TH being placed in the middle to keep CHI apart from the endings INN and EAMAID which begin with vowels.

CHITHINN NA GILLEAN RI GOID NAN UBHAL ANNS AN UBHALGHORT GED NACH FHAICEADH (or FAICEADH) IAD CO BHA A' DEANAMH FAIRE ORRA. I could see the boys stealing (of) the apples in the orchard although they couldn't see who was watching them.

GOID! (guj) steal! GOID, stealing. UBHAL-GHORT (ooal-GHorst) 1. orchard. FAIRE (fara first 'a' short) 2. watch.

CHITHEADH TU GU TRIC E LE ORD 'NA LAIMH GED NACH FHAICEADH TU E A' DEANAMH DAD A DH'OBAIR, You would see him often with a hammer in his hand though you wouldn't see him doing a tap of work. (A DH is DE DE becoming DE DH and A DH).

We are quite familiar with the use of the word of command in phrases such as DEAN DO GHNO-THACH AGUS NA CUIR A LETH-TAOBH E. Do your work and don't put it aside.

A LETH-TAOBH (a lay-toov: stress on 'lay'), to one side, really 'to a half side'.

THOIRIBH AN AIRE, A CHLANN, NACH TUIT SIBH ANNS AN UISGE. Take care children that you do not fall in the water.

16

But commands or requests can take other forms than these: for instance SGRIOBHAM AN LITIR SIN DUIT, Let me write that letter for you.

FAICEAM NA THA ANNS A' MHAILEID, Let me see what is in the bag.

This new form is got by putting -AM (or -EAM if the last vowel is I) to the end of the word of command. MAILEID (**mal-ej**) 2. bag, wallet.

Consider now these: DEANAMAID SUIDHE AN SEO AGUS CUIREAMAID AN SGAILEAN-GREINE OS AR CIONN. Let us sit here and put the sunshade over our head. SGAILEAN-GREINE (**skalan grayn-a**) 1. sunshade. INNSEADH AM BALACH SEO MAR THACHAIR AGUS FANADH AN FHEADHAINN EILE NAN TOSD. Let this boy tell how (or, the manner) it happened and let the others remain silent. 'NAN TOSD, in their silence. TOSD, 1. silence.

From the above you will observe that in speaking of ourselves we add -AMAID (or -EAMAID) to the word of command and in speaking of others -ADH (or -EADH).

Note CHI not only stands for shall (or will) see but also for, see just now, e.g. CHI MI AM BATA, I see the boat. Further, there is no -EAS form. MA CHI MI, If I shall see: never CHITHEAS.

Faclair

RI DHEANAMH (**ree yayn-av**), to be done. REUBALACH (**ray-bulach**) 1. a rebel. G'AM (GU AM) FAICINN (**gam feCHk-ing**) to see them. lit. to their seeing. SMAOIN also SMUAIN (**smooin**) 2. thought. COMHNUICH! (**kO-neeCH**) dwell!: COMHNUIDH (**kO-nee**) dwelling. TREUD (**trayd**) 1. flock. SOCRACH (**soCHk-raCH**) leisurely. FEAR-SEOLAIDH (**fer shol-ee**) 1. manager, 'boss'. MAR, how, the way that. DEIREADH (**jay-ruGH**) 1. end. SEACHDUIN (**sheCHk-in**) 2. week. GABH AIR (**gav er**) punish. ANMOCH (**ana-moCH**) late. MU'N CUAIRT (**moong cooirsht**) around. MA TA, well, then. MAR SIN LEIBH (**mar shin layv**) lit. like that with you, the same.

Gaelic to English

Faic nach dean thu a rithist e. Faiceamaid na tha
ri dheanamh fhathast. Na cluinneam facal eile as do
bheul. Na gabhadh e gnothach ris. Chi mi a' ghrian
gu h-ard anns an speur. Chi sinn am maireach thu.
An uair a chunnaic na reubalaich na saighdearan a'
tighinn, theich iad. Theid mi g'am faicinn an nochd.
Dh'fhalbh e gun ar faicinn. Ged nach faiceamaid ar
caraid tuilleadh, bidh e daonnan 'nar smaointean. An
uair a bha mi a' comhnuidh an Diura, chithinn an
ciobair air ceann a threuda a' dol gu socrach do'n
mhonadh. Ma chi thu am fear-seolaidh am maireach,
innis dha mar thachair. Mur faic sibh mi aig deireadh
na seachduine, chi sibh mi gu cinnteach air maduinn
Di-luain. Ma chi mi sibh a rithist anns an ubhalghart
gabhaidh mi oirbh leis an t-slait. Am faca sibh fear
a' bhainne a' mhaduinn seo? Chan fhaca. Mur 'eil
e tinn, is coltach gum faic sinn e na's anmoiche 'san
la a' dol mu'n cuairt mar is abhaist. Gabhaibh mo
lethsgeul, a bhean uasal. Slan leibh ma ta. Mar sin
leibh.

Translation

See that you don't do it again. Let us see what is
still to be done. Don't let me hear another word out
your mouth. Let him not take to do with it. I see
the sun high up in the sky. We shall see you to-
morrow. When the rebels saw the soldiers coming,
they fled. I shall go to see them to-night. He went
off without seeing us. Though we should see our
friend no more, he will always be in our thoughts.
When I was staying in Jura, I used to see the shepherd
at the head of his flock going leisurely to the uplands.
If you see the manager to-morrow, tell him what
happened. If you don't see me at the end of the week,
you will certainly see me on Monday morning. If I
see you again in the orchard, I'll give you a thrashing
with the stick. Did you see the milk-man this
morning? I did not. Unless he is sick, it's likely we
shall see him later in the day going around as usual.
Excuse me, lady. Good-bye then. Good-bye.

LESSON 35

AS we saw in Lesson 30 a phrase such as The house was built was translated by CHAIDH AN TAIGH A THOGAIL, meaning, word for word, as you will remember, The house went to building. We could also have put it thus, BHA AN TAIGH AIR A THOGAIL, these words meaning, The house was after its building. AIR, as we have explained before, should really be IAR, after, a word which has passed out of use unfortunately. There is still another way of translating our sentence, namely THOGADH AN TAIGH. THOGADH is formed from THOG, built, with -ADH added. In like manner we have BHRIS-EADH AN UINNEAG, The window was broken. This time EADH was added because the last vowel of BHRIS was I. Here are a few examples:

THUGADH DUAIS DO'N GHILLE, The boy was given a prize, or a prize was given to the boy.

AN DO CHUIREADH AM PAISDE DO'N SGOIL? Was the child sent to school?

DH'OLADH DEOCH-SLAINTE, A toast was drunk. DEOCH-SLAINTE (joch slan-chay) 2. toast. SLAINTE, 2. health.

NACH DO DH'AISIGEADH AN LEABHAR? Was the book not handed back?

DO DH'AISIGEADH could also be written D'AISIGEADH (dashig-uGH). AISIG! (ashig) deliver, hand back, ferry across.

In Future time -AR or -EAR is added instead of -AIDH or -IDH.

TOGAR AN TAIGH, The house will be built.

BRISEAR AN UINNEAG, The window will be broken.

OLAR DEOCH-SLAINTE, A toast will be drunk.

FEUMAR AN TAIGH A LEAGADH, It will be necessary to demolish the house, or The house will need to be demolished.

FEUM (faym) need, must: FEUMAR, will be needed. LEAG! (lyayk) knock down! demolish!

We could also have said, THEID AN TAIGH A THOGAIL (leagadh), BIDH AN TAIGH AIR A THOGAIL (leagadh). The house will be built. The house will be demolished.

The 'should be' and 'would be' forms are much the same as the 'should' and 'would' forms only that -TEADH is the ending instead of -ADH or -EADH. Thus THOGADH, would lift or build, THOGTEADH, would be lifted or built. BHRISEADH, would break, BHRISTEADH, would be broken. CHITHEADH, would see, CHITEADH (CHee-chuGH) would be seen.

BHUAILTEADH THU LEIS A' BHALL NAN DEANADH TU SEASAMH AN SIN, You would be hit with the ball if you would stand there. BALL (ba-ool) 1. ball: also member.

THA E COLTACH GUN CUIRTEADH AIR FALBH E NAN DEANADH E A LEITHID DE RUD. It is likely he would be sent away if he would do such a thing. Note that with the 'would' forms we use TU for thou, and THU with the 'would be' forms.

LEITHID (lyay-hij) like. A LEITHID SIN, the like of that.

DH'OLTEADH IOMADH DEOCH-SLAINTE MU'N ROBH AN OIDHCHE SEACHAD, Many a toast would be drunk before the night went past

CHAN IARRTEADH ORRA MAL A PHAID-EADH AIR TALAMH CHO GARBH, They wouldn't be asked to pay rent on ground so rough.

If an action word has two forms, remember always to use the first after MA, GED, NA (all that or what) and A, and the second form after GUN (GUM) NACH, CHA, AN (AM), NAN (NAM), MU e.g GED A CHITHEAR NA'S TRICE ANN AN GLASCHU E ANNS NA LAITHEAN A THA RI TIGHINN, (or TEACHD) CHA CHREID MI GUM FAICEAR A RITHIST E ANNS AN TAIGH SEO.

Though he will be seen more often in Glasgow in days to come, I don't think he will be seen again in this house.

There are some expressions in Gaelic over which the student might puzzle long enough without finding out their exact meaning. Here is one. It is the word SAOIL (**sooil**) meaning, Think, suppose, fancy or imagine. A few examples will make its use clear.

SHAOIL IAD NACH FALBHADH AM BATA AGUS AN T-SID CHO DONA, They imagined that the boat would not depart and the weather so bad. SID (**sheej**) 2. weather, good or bad.

SHAOILEADH DUINE GUN ROBH E AS A BHEACHD: One would think that he was out of his senses.

SAOILIDH MI AIR DOIGH GUM BHEIL AN STUADH DIREACH AGUS AIR DOIGH EILE GUM BHEIL I CAM: I fancy in a way that the gable is upright and in another way that it is bent. STUADH (**stoo-uGH**) 2. gable of house ; billow. CAM, bent, curved ; also, blind of an eye.

SAOIL SIBH AN SIL E? Do you think it will rain? Note how the 'AN', the sign of a question was dropped before SAOIL.

CHA TIG E AN NOCHD, SAOIL THU? He will not come to-night, what do you think?

AN TEID SINN DHACHAIDH? SAOIL THU FHEIN? Shall we go home? What do you think yourself?

SAOIL THUSA C'AR SON NACH D'THAINIG E? Can you imagine (think what his reason was) why he did not come?

SAOIL AM BI UAIR MHATH AGAINN? I wonder if we shall get good weather? UAIR (**oo-ir**) 2. hour, weather. Notice how SAOIL by itself translates the English 'I wonder'.

SAOIL C'AIT' AM BHEIL E A NIS? I wonder where he is now?

SAOIL DE THA E A' DEANAMH AN DRASDA? I wonder what he is doing at present?

SAOIL CO BHA AN SEO? I wonder who was here?

SAOIL AN TIG E AN DIUGH? I wonder if he will come to-day?

CHA CHREID MI GUN TIG, I don't think (believe) he will come.

CHA CHREID MI NACH TIG, I don't think that he will not come, i.e. I believe he will come. Notice this peculiar type of answer. It is very common in Gaelic. We could also have said SAOILIDH MI GUN TIG. I fancy he will come.

Another common expression is THA FHIOS which may be translated by 'of course', 'surely'. THA FHIOS (ha-eess).

THA AN DUINE SIN SEOLTA. That man is cute ('fly'). THA FHIOS GUM BHEIL. Of course he is. NACH 'EIL FHIOS AIG A H-UILE DUINE AIR SIN? Surely everyone knows that.

AN RUITH NA H-EICH AN DIUGH? Will the horses run to-day? THA FHIOS GUN RUITH. Of course they will. NACH 'EIL FHIOS GUN RUITH? Surely they will, i.e. What's going to hinder them? Why shouldn't they?

Faclair

GU MATH DHETH (**goo ma yay**) well-off. SEALBH (**shel-uv**) 1. fortune, possessions. CUIDEACHD-OLA (**kooj-aCHd Ola**) 2. oil-company. BOCSA (**bOksa**) 1. box. MARGADH (**marug-uGH**) 1. market. LETH-UAIR (**lyay-oor**) half-an-hour. CUNNTAS (**koon-tas**) 1. account, SEID! (**shayj**) blow! CEAD (**kayd**) 1. leave, permission. CEILEAR (**kay-lar**) 1. warbling. MOCHTHRATH (**moCH-ra**) 1. dawn: very early. AS LETH (**ass lay**) regarding, to account of, on behalf of. CUIR AS LETH, impute ; DEAN SIN AS MO LETH, do that on my behalf. BATH! (**ba**) drown! CUAN MOR (**kooan mOr**) Atlantic Ocean. GIN, person or thing. DH'FHAOIDTE (**Ghoo-chay**) perhaps. DEOCH LAIDIR (**joch la-jir**) 2. strong-drink. MUR B'E, unless it were . NEO-BHLASDA (**nyo-vlasda**) without taste, insipid. OLTE (for OLTEADH): ADH often left out.

Saoil thu an tig e an nochd? Tha fhios gun tig. Am bheil iad gu math dheth, saoil sibh? Cha chreid mi gum bheil. Chaill iad a' chuid bu mhotha d'an sealbh ann an cuideachd-ola. An tog thu am bocsa seo? Tha fhios gun tog. Nach 'eil fhios gun tog. Bidh margadh a' chruidh ann am maireach. Am bi thusa ann? Tha fhios gum bi. Nach 'eil fhios gum bi. Saoil c'uin' a rainig iad? Mu leth-uair an deidh naoi an nochd. Saoil thu am paigh e an cunntas sin? Cha chreid mi gum paigh. Cha chreid mi nach paigh ceart gu leoir. Saoil de tha 'ga chumail. Chan 'eil fhios aig duine.

Cha deanar cron sam bith air a' phaisde. Togar na siuil an uair a sheideas a' ghaoth. Cha chreid mi gun cuirear air falbh e mu'n till am maighstir fhein. Thugadh a chead dha. Rinneadh eathar beag as a' chraoibh sin. Dh' iarradh e gu banais. Chluinnteadh ceilear nan eun anns a' mhochthrath mu'n eireadh a' ghrian. Thuirt e nach cuirteadh as a leth gum bu mheirleach e. Nach do bhathadh iad anns a' chuan mhor? Bhathadh a h-uile gin dhiubh. Dh' fhaoidte nach fhaicear a rithist e. Chan olte uiread de dheoch laidir anns an tir sin mur b'e gun robh an t-uisge cho neo-bhlasda.

Translation

Do you think he will come to-night? Of course he will. Are they well-off, do you think? I don't think they are. They lost the most of their fortune in an oil company. Will you lift this box? Yes, of course. Surely I would do that. The cattle-market will be on to-morrow. Will you be there? Of course I shall. You may be sure I'll be there. I wonder when they arrived? About half-past nine to-night. Do you think he will pay that account? I don't think he will. I think he'll pay all right. I wonder what's keeping him? No one knows.

No harm will be done to the child. The sails will be hoisted when the wind blows. I don't think he'll be put away before the master himself returns. He got his leave (got dismissed). A little boat was made out of that tree. He was asked to a wedding. The warbling of the birds could be heard in the early morning before the sunrise. He said that it would not be imputed to him that he was a thief. Were they not drowned in the ocean? Yes, every one of them. Perhaps he won't be seen again. There would not be so much strong-drink drunk in that land were it not that the water is so insipid.

LESSON 36

IAIN: AN D' FHUAIR THU AIR AIS AN T-AIRGIOD A CHUIR THU ANNS A' GHNOTH-ACH SIN?

SEUMAS: CHA D' FHUAIR. FHUAIR MI NA PHAIDHEAS AM MAL AGUS NA CISEAN.

Iain: Did you get back the money you put into that business?

James: No. I got what will pay the rent and taxes.

CIS (**keesh**) 2. tax.

In the above dialogue we see how FHUAIR, got or found, is variously used. Remember that GED, although; MA, if; and A, the person or thing that, never put in a DO for past time.

From FHUAIR we have FHUARADH (**hooar-uGH**) meaning, was or were found or got. Note how an 'i' has been dropped in FHUARADH. Very often we have FHUARAS (**hooar-as**). FHUARAS AN LAOGH ANNS AN ARBHAR, The calf was found in the corn. ARBHAR (**arav-ar**) 1. standing corn. LAOGH (**looGH**) 1. calf.

Now from FAIGH! (**fa-ee**) find! get! we would have expected DH' FHAIGH instead of FHUAIR, and FAIGHIDH for shall or will get, find. Instead we have GHEIBH (**yev**) shall or will get, find: also GHEIBHEADH (**yevuGH**) would get, find. The FAIGH forms are not lost, however. They are used as 'second' forms after AN (AM), CHA, NACH etc. GED, MA and A take the 'first' forms always, e.g. MA GHEIBH MI, If I get. There is no -EAS form.

FIACH GUM FAIGH THU AM PAIPEAR-FEASGAIR DHOMH, IAIN. See that you get the evening-paper for me, Iain. GHEIBH MI SIN DHUIBH, ATHAR. I'll get that for you, father.

GHEIBHEAR FUASGLADH DO'N CHEIST SIN UAIR-EIGIN ACH CHAN FHAIGHEAR E 'NAR LATHA FHEIN. A solution will be found to that question some time, but it won't be found in our own day. FUASGLADH (**fooas-gluGH**) 1. solution ; also relief.

GED GHEIBHEADH SIBH GACH NI A DH' AINMICH MI, CHAN FHAIGHEADH SIBH MORAN TOILEACHAS-INNTINN AS. Though you would get all that I mentioned, you would not get much satisfaction out of it. TOILEACHAS-INNTINN (**tolaCH-as een-ching**) 1. satisfaction.

CHAN FHAIGHTEADH A LEITHID EILE AIR SON OLCAIS ANNS AN TIR, Another like him for badness couldn't be found in the country. A LEITHID EILE (**a lay-hij ayla**) lit. his like else, another like him. AN LEITHID EILE, Another like them. AIR SON (**er son**) for, on account (of). OLCAS, 1. badness.

As well as FAOTAINN (**foot-ing**) getting, another form FAIGHINN (**fa-ying**) is sometimes used. THA E A' FAOTAINN (FAIGHINN) NA THOILL E, He is getting what he deserved. TOILL! (**toyll**) deserve! THAINIG IAD A DH' FHAOTAINN NAN LEABHRAICHEAN, They came to get (lit. to getting of) the books ; but BU TOIGH LEO NA LEABHRAICHEAN FHAOTAINN, They would like to get the books. In the first of these two sentences, the English order of the words is kept because A DH' FHAOTAINN NAN LEABHRAICHEAN expresses the purpose of the coming. In the second, no purpose is expressed and the order is reversed in Gaelic: hence NA LEABHRAICHEAN FHAOTAINN. Again in the first, the DO (now worn down to A) has been doubled, thus A DH'. Compare THA MI A' DOL A DH'EIRINN, I am going to Eire. In the second sentence the A' is usually dropped.

The student often finds difficulty with sentences expressing some condition or other. Consider the following :

NAM PAIDHEADH E A MHAL, CHA CHAILL-EADH E A THAIGH, If he would pay his rent, he would not lose his house. PAIDH! (**pa-ee**) pay!

NAN DO PHAIDH E A MHAL, CHA CHAILL-EADH E A THAIGH, If he had paid his rent, he would not have lost his house.

Or again, MUR BIODH GUN DO PHAIDH E A MHAL, BHA E AIR A THAIGH A CHALL, If he hadn't paid his rent he would have lost (lit. was after losing) his house. NAN DO CHAILL THU AN TAIGH, BHITHINN GLE DHUILICH, If you had lost the house I would have been very sorry. MUR B'E, were it not that, could have replaced MUR BIODH.

From these last two sentences we see that PHAIDH and CHAILL can have respectively the meanings of HAD PAID and HAD LOST as well as PAID and LOST ; also CHAILLEADH can mean WOULD HAVE LOST as well as WOULD LOSE.

MUR BIODH GUN D' THAINIG THU AN RATHAD SEO, BHIODH E MARBH, If you hadn't come this way, he would have died.

MUR BIODH GUN D' THAINIG THU AN RATHAD SEO, BHA E AIR A BHI MARBH, If you hadn't come this way, he had died (or would have died).

NAN DEANADH TU SIN, DHEANADH TU COMAIN MHOR ORM ; also NAN D'RINN THU SIN, CHUIREADH TU COMAIN MHOR ORM, both meaning if you would have done (or had done) that, you would have much obliged me ; or again NAN DEANADH TU SIN, CHUIREADH THU COMAIN MHOR ORM, same meaning as last. CUIR COMAIN AIR, oblige. COMAIN (komen) 2. obligation. DEAN COMAIN AIR! oblige him!

BHITHINN AN SEO AN DE MUR BIODH GUN DO CHUM AN STOIRM MI, I should have been here yesterday if the storm had not kept me, i.e. if it would not have been that the storm kept me.

One small point more. These Should and Would forms often carry the meaning of Could as for example CHLUINNEADH SIBH NA H-EOIN A' SEINN ANNS A' CHOILLE. You could hear (or could have heard) the birds singing in the wood.

Faclair

GEANNAIR (**gen-ner**) 1. small hammer. SITH (**shee**) 2. peace. A BHEAG (**a vek**) any, or but little according to sentence. LA SAOR, free day or holiday. A DHITH (**a ye**) wanting. LEAN! (**lyen**) follow! continue! TRUSGAN-SAMHRAIDH: TRUSGAN (**troos-gan**) 1. clothes. SAMHRADH (**saooruGH**) 1. summer. SAMHRAIDH, of summer. FAILTE (**fa-eel-cha**) 2. welcome. FURAN (**fooran**) 1. hospitality. UAIR SAM BITH (**ooir sam be**) anytime. DUINE SAM BITH, anyone. TOGAIR! (**tOgir**) wish! COR (**kor**) 1. condition. AN IMPIS (**an eempish**) just about, on point of. CIALL (**keeal**) 2. reason, sense. BU LEIR DHITH (**boo layr ye**) twas evident to her. IS LEIR DHOMH, I can see (object or idea). LEANABH (**lyenuv**) 1. child. AODANN (**oo-dan**) 1. face; also AGHAIDH. GABH ORAN, sing a song. CISEAN (**keeshan**) 1. hamper. CIUIN (**kyooin**) calm, gentle. GU SOCAIR (**goo soCH-kir**) gently. BUAILTEACH (**booil-chaCH**) liable. THUGAD! (**hook-ad**) get out of the way! look out! FIADHAICH (**fee-uGH-eeCH**) wild, fierce. FEUM (**faym**) 1. use, need, necessity. MAIR! (**mar**) last! continue.

Gaelic to English

Faigh dhomh an geannair, a Sheumais. Chan 'eil sinn a' faotainn (or a' faighinn) moran sith anns a' chearn seo de'n bhaile. Cha dean e a bheag de mhath a nis ged gheibheamaid uair mhath agus ar laithean saora seachad. Cha d' fhuair mi as cho saor. Gheibheadh iad na bha a dhith orra nan gabhadh iad e. Ma mhaireas an uair mhath, gheibh sinn ar trusgan-samhraidh roimh fhada. Faodaidh sibh a bhi cinnteach gum faigh sibh failte agus furan uair sam bith a thogras sibh tighinn an rathad seo. Cha chreid mi gum faighear duine sam bith a tha toilichte le cor an t-saoghail an drasda. Mur faighteadh an lighiche cho deas, bha an duine truagh air a bhi marbh. Nan glaisteadh an dorus cha d' fhuair (or chan fhaigheadh), am meirleach a steach. Nan d'

rinn e sud, gheibheadh e a dhuais. Bha am
boirionnach an impis a ciall a chall an uair a bu leir
dhith nach faigheadh i a leanabh air ais a rithist.
Falbh agus nigh d' aodann, a bhalaich. Nach e a
tha salach. An sgriobhadh tu cho math (ri) sin?
Ghabhainnse oran cho math dhuit. Fiach gun dean
sibh cabhag a nis. Leigibh an cisean gu socair sios.
Tha na soitheachan a th' ann an diugh buailteach air
briseadh. Thugad! Buailidh e thu. Tha e fiadhaich.
Bhuail e clach orm anns a' cheann. Cuir seachad na
leabhraichean sin. Chan 'eil moran feum orra, is e
mo bheachd.

Translation

Get me the small hammer, James. We are not
getting much peace in this quarter of the town. It
won't do any (of) good now though we should get
good weather and our holidays past. I did not get
away (out of it) so freely. They would get what they
wanted if they would take it. If the good weather
continues we shall get our summer-wear before long.
You may be certain that you will get a generous
welcome any time that you please to come this way.
I don't think anyone will be found that is pleased
with the state of the world at present. If the doctor
had not been found so readily the poor fellow would
have been dead. If the door had been locked the
thief would not have got in. If he had done that,
he would have got his reward. The woman was on
the point of losing her reason when it became clear
to her that she would not get her child back again.
Away and wash your face, boy. Isn't it dirty. Could
you write as well as that? I could sing a song as
well for you. See that you hurry up now. Lay the
hamper down quietly. The vessels of to-day (or
present-day ships) are liable to break. Look out!
He'll hit you. He is wild. He struck me on the head
with a stone (note Gaelic rendering). Put away those
books. They are not much use in my opinion.

LESSON 37

WE have used the word THUG very often in past lessons. It can mean Gave or Took or Brought according to the words which follow.

THUG E A CHEAD DO'N SGALAIG, He gave the farm servant his leave. CEAD (**kayd**) 1. leave, permission. SGALAG (**skal-ag**) 2. farm servant.

AN D'THUG IAD LEO AN COTAICHEAN? Did they take (or bring) with them their coats?

MUR D'THUG, FHUAIR IAD NA FRASAN, If they didn't, they got the showers. D'THUG (**dook**) short for DO THUG.

THUGADH NA PRIOSANAICH FA CHOMHAIR A' CHEANNAIRD, The prisoners were brought in front of the commander. THUGADH (**hook-uGH**) were (or was) brought. CEANNARD (**kyan-ard**). 1. commander. FA CHOMHAIR (**fa-CHor**) before, in front of, followed by 'of' form. Now the word of command is THOIR! (**ho-ir**) give! take! bring! (it is found as TABHAIR! (**tav-ir**) sometimes); but this is one of the few action-words that are not regular and so we should not be surprised when we see THUG for past-time and BHEIR (**vayr**) for future-time. Study the following examples carefully.

THOIR DEOCH DO'N GHILLE! Give the boy a drink!

AN TOIR SIBH CEUM AN RATHAD SEO, A BHEAN UASAL? Will you step this way, madam?

BHEIR, GU TOILEACH, I shall, with pleasure.

Notice how we said AN TOIR and not AN THOIR. TOIR (**to-ir**).

MA BHEIR MI MILSEAG DHUIT, UILLEIM, AN GABH THU ORAN DUINN? If I give you a sweetie, William, will you sing a song to us?

DH' FHAOIDTE(ADH) GUN GABH, Perhaps I will. Is also written DH' FHAOIDTE.

30

DH'FHAOIDTEADH (**GHoo-chay**), perhaps, it might be. MILSEAG (**meel-shag**) 2. sweetie.

GABH ORAN, sing a song, is perhaps better than SEINN ORAN. SEINN is also used for a musical instrument although it is quite commonly used for singing. There is no -EAS form for BHEIR and so we say MA BHEIR and not MA BHEIREAS. From BEIR (**bayr**) catch! however, we get MA BHEIREAS MI etc., If I etc. catch.

BHEIREAR DUAISEAN DO NA GILLEAN A THA DEANADACH, Rewards will be given to the boys that are industrious. DEANADACH (**jana-daCH**) industrious, diligent.

CHA CHREID MI GUN TOIREAR MORAN BUANNACHD AS A' GHNOTHACH UD, I don't think much profit will be taken out of that business. TOIREAR (**torar**) will be taken. BUANNACHD (**booan-naCHk**) 2. profit.

The 'should' and 'would' forms require a little attention. Thus we have BHEIREADH E for He (or it) would take or give with the two special forms BHEIRINN (**vayring**) I should give, take, and BHEIREAMAID (**vayr-a-mij**), We should or would take, give. But after AM (AN), CHA, NACH etc. the forms we use are made up from either of the two words TOIR and TUG and so we get TOIREADH and TUGADH. These also have the special forms in -INN (AINN) and EAMAID (AMAID).

BHEIRINN NOT DUIT NAN TOIREADH (TUGADH) TU NA CLACHAN SEO AIR FALBH, I would give you a pound if you would take these stones away.

CHA TOIRINN AIR FALBH IAD GED BHEIR-EADH SIBH NOT DHOMH, I wouldn't take them away though you should give me a pound. NOT (**not**) 1. pound (in money).

AN TUGADH TU UIREAD AIRGID AIR AN FHAINNE SIN? Would you give as much (of) money for (on) that ring?

BHEIREADH, AGUS A DHA UIREAD, I would and twice that amount. UIREAD (**oorad**) 1. as (or so) much (amount) A DHA (**a GHa**) two times.

Note that in answers the special forms in -AINN (INN) and AMAID (EAMAID) are usually dropped in favour of those ending in -ADH (-EADH) but may be used in replies for emphasis.

CHA B' ANN GUN SPAIRN MHOR A BHEIR-TEADH TORADH AS AN DROCH FHEARANN SIN, It wasn't without a great struggle that produce could have been got (taken) out of that poor land. TORADH (tor-uGH) 1. produce. SPAIRN (sparn) 2. great exertion. BHEIRTEADH (vayr-chuGH) could be or have been taken.

DROCH (droCH) bad, and DEAGH (jayoo) good, come before the name-word and sharpen, if possible, its first letter. FEARANN (fer-an) 1. land.

CHA TOIRTEADH NA SOCHAIREAN SIN AIR FALBH NAN D' RINN IAD DEAGH BHUIL DHIUBH, These benefits would not have been taken away if they had made good use of them. BUIL (bool) 2. use ; consequence.

From O meaning 'from' when joined up with MI, TU etc. we get UAM (ooam) from me: UAIT (ooich) from thee: UAIDH (ooee) from him or it: UAIPE (ooee-pa) from her or it: UAINN (oo-ing) from us: UAIBH (oo-iv) from you: UAPA (ooa-pa) from them. Often we find from BHO (vo), BHUAM (vooam) from me: BHUAIT (voo-ich) from thee, etc. NA TOIR MO LASADAIN BHUAM, Don't take my matches from me. LASADAN (lassa-dan) 1. match. Note: seldom NA THOIR.

In the same way, from AS (ass) meaning out of, along with MI, TU, etc. we form ASAM (assam) out of me: ASAD (assad) out of thee: AS (ass) out of him (or it): AISTE (ash-chay) out of her (or it): ASAINN (ass-ing) out of us: ASAIBH (ass-iv) out of you: ASTA (ass-ta) out of them.

THOIR and the different forms of this action-word are used to form many common phrases.

THOIR AN RATHAD, AN DORUS, AN LEAB-AIDH, AM BAILE, etc. ORT! Take the road. Go to the door. Go to bed. Go to town, etc.

THUG E AN CAR AS AN DUINE, He took the twist out of (i.e. cheated) the man. CAR, 1. twist.

THUG IAD NA BUINN ASTA, They took the soles of the feet out of them (i.e. they bolted) BONN (ba-oon) 1. sole of foot. BUINN (boo-ing) soles.

BHA E A' TOIRT TAMAILT DAIBH, He was giving offence to them. TAMAILT (tam-ilch) 2. offence.

THOIR FAINEAR! NOTICE! FAINEAR (fa-nyer) under observation.

THOIR AS E! Take (drink) it up (out)!

THOIR AN AIRE! (ar-a) Pay attention!

THOIR FIOS DO! Inform! Give information to!

THUG E ORM COISEACHD AIR A BHEUL-AOBH, He made me (brought on me) walk in front of him.

A THOIRT A MACH, to bring out, i.e. to gain or reach. Also to gain a victory. THUG E A MACH A' BHUAIDH, He gained the victory. BUAIDH (boo-ay) 2. victory.

Note these three phrases carefully:

DH'FHIACH E AM FEARANN A THOIRT A MACH, He tried to take out the land (i.e. to reach the land).

DH'FHIACH E A THOIRT A MACH, He tried to reach it (the land) i.e. its taking out.

THOG SINN FEARANN, We sighted land.

Faclair

GUN ROBH MATH AGAD (AGAIBH) pr. ' Goon ro maa-gad ' with stress on 'maa'. Thank you: Also TAPADH LEAT (LEIBH). FION DEARG 1. Port wine. BIADH! (be-uGH) feed! BIADHADH (be-uGHuGH) feeding. BARRACHD (bar-raCHk) 2. excess, more, followed by 'of' forms. A (DE) BHARRACHD, extra. TIGHINN BHUAIDH, to come from it, get over it. DOMHAIL (do-it) (also DUMHAIL) thick, bulky, crowded. UIDHEAM-TURUIS (oo-yum toor-ish) 2. luggage, baggage. LUCHD-TATHAICH (looCHk ta-eeCH) visitors. LUCHD, people. TATHAICH! visit! RANNSAICH! (raoonseeCH) explore! search! RANNSACHADH (raoon-saCH-uGH) 1. exploring, examining, searching.

RIARACHADH (reer-aCH-uGH), 1. satisfaction. MU
DHEIREADH (moo yayr-uGH) final, at last. LUATH
(looa) 2. ashes. BRAT-URLAIR (brat oor-ler) 1.
carpet. PEANN-LUAIDHE (pyaoon looay-a) 1. lead-
pencil. LUAIDH (looay) 1. lead. SUATHAN (sooa-
han) 1. rubber. BUIN! (boon) belong! CUDTHROM-
ACH (coodrum-aCH) important. SEOLADH (shol-
uGH) 1. direction, address. EOLAS (yolas) 1. knowledge, acquaintance. FEUMAIL (faym-il) necessary,
useful. IMICH! (eem-eeCH) depart! BRAIGH-
GHILL (bra-yeel) 2. pre-eminence. MNATHAN (mra-
han) women. BANAS-TAIGHE (ban-as ta-ee) 2.
housewifery, household-management.

Gaelic to English

Thug i air Seumas suidhe. Thoir leat do chota.
Thoir a steach an cu. Thoir an sgian o'n phaisde.
Thoir dhomh deoch bhainne, ma's e do thoil e. Seo
a nis. Gun robh math agad. Nach math am fion
dearg sin. Thoir as e. Thug i uine mhor a' biadhadh
nan cearc. Cha toir a' chlann an aire do na tha mi
ag radh riutha. An toireadh sibh coig notaichean air
a' chu seo? Is mi nach toireadh. Bheirinn tri
notaichean air. Cha toirinn sgillinn a bharrachd. Tha
Mairi Ruadh gle bhochd an drasda ach faodaidh i
tighinn bhuaidh. Thug i a seomar fein oirre.
Bheireadh e an car as athair fhein. An d' thug sibh
fainear co dha a bha e a' toirt an airgid? Cha d'
thug, ach bheir mi air, an t-airgiod a thoirt air ais.
B' fhearr duit na buinn a thoirt asad cho luath agus
is urrainn duit. Nan tugainn tamailt do neach sam
bith, is mi a bhitheadh gle dhuilich. Leis cho
domhail agus a bha an ceo, cha b' urrainn do'n
sgioba an tir a thoirt a mach. Am bi sibh cho math
agus (or, a's) mo chuidheachadh le m' uidheam turuis.
Ni mi sin gu toileach. Thugadh cead do'n luchd-
tathaich laraichean a' chaisteil a rannsachadh.
Faodaidh mi a radh gun d' thug an dealbh mu
dheireadh barrachd riarachaidh dhomh na iad uile.
Feumaidh tu deagh aire a thoirt nach leig thu le
luath do phioba tuiteam air a' bhrat-urlair. Ma

bhuineas am peann-luaidhe agus an suathan dhi, na toir bhuaipe iad. Is iomadh rud cudthromach air nach toirear iomradh anns na leabhraichean eachdraidh. Bheirear gach seoladh agus gach eolas feumail duibh mu'n imich sibh. Thug i braigh-ghill air mnathan a' bhaile 'na banas-taighe.

Translation

She made James sit down. Take your coat with you. Bring in the dog. Take the knife from the child. Give me a drink of milk if you please. Here it is now. Thank you. Isn't that port good. Drink it up (out). She spent (took) a long time feeding the hens. The children will not pay attention to what I am saying to them. Would you give five pounds for this dog? I certainly would not. ('Tis I that wouldn't). I would give three pounds for it. I wouldn't give a penny more. Red-haired Mary is very poorly just now but she may get over it. She went to her own room. He would cheat his own father. Did you notice to whom he was giving the money? I didn't, but I'll make him hand back the money. It would be better for you to clear out as quickly as you can. If I should give offence to anyone I indeed would be very sorry. With the mist being so thick it was not possible for the crew to reach the land. Will you be so good as help me with my luggage? I'll do that with pleasure. The visitors were given leave to explore the ruins of the castle. I may say that the last picture gave me more satisfaction than them all. You must take great care that you do not allow your pipe-ash to fall on the carpet. If the pencil and rubber belong to her, don't take them from her. There is many an important matter that will not get mention in the history books. All directions and information necessary will be given to you before you depart. She excelled the women of the town in her housewifery.

LESSON 38

SAOIL AN CLUINN SINN BHUAIDH IDIR? I
wonder if (or do you think that) we will hear from
him at all? is a question that is sometimes asked
regarding a friend who has gone away. BHUAIDH
(vooay) from him. The reply might be CLUINNIDH
SINN AN DRASDA AGUS A RITHIST, We'll hear
now and again ; or again perhaps CHA CHLUINN
ACH AIR UAIRIBH. We won't hear but occasionally. AIR UAIRIBH (er ooriv) occasionally. Now
CLUINN! (klooing) hear! is the word of command
and you would expect CHLUINN in past time.
Though this is sometimes used we generally have
CHUALA (CHooa-la), and CUALA (kooa-la) without
the usual DO before it after AN (AM), CHA, NACH
etc. AN CUALA TU AN NAIGHEACHD? CHA
CHUALA. DE THA A' TACHAIRT A NIS? Did
you hear the news? I didn't. What's happening now?
In passing, notice how we said TU not THU after
CUALA just as we did in AM FACA TU? Did
you see.

CHUALADH (or CHUALAS) FUAIM NAN
RAMH LE NA BAILLIDHEAN, The sound of the
oars was heard by the water-bailiffs. BAILLIDH
(bal-ye) 1. bailiff.

MA CHLUINNEAS I GUM BI E A' TIGHINN GU
LUATH BIDH I SONA, If she hears that he will be
coming soon she will be happy.

CHA CHLUINNEAR SGAL NA PIOBA ANNS A'
GHLEANN UD GU BRATH TUILLIDH, The skirl
of the pipes will nevermore be heard in yon glen.
SGAL (skal) 1. skirl, blast. GU BRATH TUILLIDH
(goo braCH tooil-ya) for evermore.

CHLUINNTEADH SGREADAIN A' BHOIRIONN-
AICH OS CIONN STRAIGHLICH NA SRAIDE,

The shrieks of the woman could be heard above the traffic-roar of the street. STRAIGHLICH (**stral-yeeCH**) 2. traffic-roar, din. SGREADAN (**skred-an**) 1. shriek.

CHA CHLUINNEADH SIBH DUINE SAM BITH 'GA CHAINEADH, You wouldn't hear anybody speaking ill of him. CAIN! (**ka-in**) disparage!

BU MHATH LEAM AN ORAID SIN A CHLUINNTINN, I would like to hear that speech. IS MATH LEAM, I think good, I like. BU MHATH LEAM, 'Twere good with me, I would like ; also I liked (in past time). ORAID (**or-ij**) 2. speech. BU MHATH LEAM A CLUINNTINN, I would like to hear it (or her), literally Its or her hearing. BU MHATH LEAM DO CHLUINNTINN, I would like to hear you ; and so on.

We could also have used BU TOIGH LEAM for I would like or I liked. TOIGH (**to-ee**) pleasing. TOIGHEACH AIR (**toee-aCH**) keen, fond of.

Now consider the following ways in which we may show purpose. Let us take the phrase, I came to hear the speech.

THAINIG MI A CHLUINNTINN NA H-ORAIDE, I came to (the) hearing of the speech.

THAINIG MI GUS AN ORAID A CHLUINN-TINN, I came in order the speech to hear.

THAINIG MI A CHUM'S GUN CLUINNINN AN ORAID, I came in order that I might hear the speech. A CHUM'S (**a CHums**) for purpose of, in order (that). GUS (**goose**) in order. But, I came to hear it (the speech) would be rendered as THAINIG MI G'A CLUINNTINN where GU (**goo**) means, to, in order to. (Before AN meaning 'the', it is written GUS). 'A' means 'its' but as it represents ORAID, Class 2. it did not sharpen the next word CLUINNTINN. Similarly, THAINIG E GU M' CHLUINNTINN, He came to hear me. THAINIG E G'AR CLUINNTINN, He came to hear us. M' is MO, my and AR, our. THA MI A'DOL G'A BHREABADH, I am going to kick it (or, him). BREAB! (**breb**) kick! Do not mix up these GU forms with the AIG forms. For instance CHAIDH E THAIRIS G'A FHAICINN, He went

37

over to see it (boat etc. Cl. 1) but BHA E 'GA
FHAICINN, He was seeing it where 'GA is short for
AIG A, at its.

A very common turn of phrase is the following.
THUG E TOILEACHEAS-INNTINN DHA, MI A
BHI SEALLTAINN CHO MATH, It gave him
satisfaction, me to be looking so well. We could also
have said THUG E TOILEACHAS-INNTINN DHA
GUN ROBH MI A' SEALLTAINN CHO MATH.
SEALL! look! SEALLTAINN (shaool-ting) looking.

Just as LE joined with MI to give LEAM, so in
the same way we have from MU (moo) about, UMAM
(oomam) about me. UMAD (oomad) about thee.
UIME (ooeem-a) about him or it. UIMPE (ooim-pa)
about her or it. UMAINN (oom-ayng) about us.
UMAIBH (oom-ayv) about you. UMPA (oom-pa)
about them.

AN ANN UMAM-SA A BHA IAD A' BRUIDH-
INN? Is it about me they were speaking?

Note the following use of BHUAM (or UAM) etc.
CIOD THA BHUAIPE? What does she want? (Lit.
What is from her?) CHAN 'EIL BHUAIPE ACH
DEOCH BHAINNE MU'N TEID I A LAIDHE, She
only wants (requires) a drink of milk before she goes
to bed. AM BHEIL NI SAM BITH UAIBH? Do
you lack anything? THA TRIUIR UAINN, We lack
(or miss) three. THA UAIBH FALBH, You had
better (or It is your duty to) go.

Faclair

DE B'AILL LEIBH? (jay baliv), What was it you
desired (to say, etc.)? I beg pardon. GABHAIBH (or
GABH) MO LEISGEUL (ga-iv mo lesh kayl) Excuse
me. RO, very, extremely. A DH' (aGH) to. AN
UIRIDH (an oor-ee) last year. GUTH (goo) 1. voice,
word. A RIAMH (a ree-uv) ever. CONNSACHADH
(kown-saCH-uGH) 1. argument. CAIN! (ka-in) revile.
traduce! MAR AN CEUDNA (mar an kaydna) likewise. AMHARUS (avar-us) 1. suspicion, doubt.
COMAIDH (komy) 2. mess. SEALBH (shel-uv) 1.
possessions, fortune. AIR TI (er chee) bent or determined on. AN IMPIS (an eem-pish) on point of.

FODHA (fo-a) under. TEARN! (charn) save! rescue!
TEARNADH (charn-uGH) saving, rescuing. CROCH!
(kroCH) hang! MARAG (mar-ag) 2. pudding.
MUINEAL (mooeen-yal) 1. neck. LABHAIR! (lav-
ir) speak! THOIR SEACHAD! give over! deliver!
GEARAIN! (ger-an) complain! GEARAN (ger-an)
1. complaint. C'AINM? (ken-im) what name? DUIT
(dooch) to you. GOBHA (gO-a) 1. smith.
GOBHAINN (gO-ing) of a smith. LE UR CEAD
(kayd) by your leave, sir. GAIRDEACHAS (garja-
CHas) 1. joy, gladness. MAR IS FHAIDE (mar iss
aja) as is further, the further. MAR A B'FHAIDE
(mara baja) the further (past time). DOIMHNEAD
(doeen-ad) 2. depth. A' DOL AN D, going into
depth, becoming deeper: so also A' DOL AN
AIRDE, going into height, becoming higher.
RUNAICH (roon-eeCH) decided. TAMULL (tam-
uil) 1. while. TRUS! (troos) gather! TRUSADH
(troos-uGH) gathering. A CHUID (a CHuj) his share
of, his. AON CHUID . . . NO (oon CHuj . . , no)
either . . . or. CAILLTE (kalchay) lost. SGRIOSTA
(skrees-ta) destroyed.

Gaelic to English

Cluinnidh mi an sgeul sin am maireach. De b'aill
leibh? Thuirt mi gun cluinninn an sgeul sin am
maireach. Gabhaibh mo leisgeul. Cha chluinn mi
gu ro mhath. An cluinn thu mi, Iain? Cluinnidh, a
mhathair. An cuala sibh dad uapa o'n dh' fhalbh iad
a dh' America an uiridh? Cha chuala mi guth a
riamh. An cuala duine a leithid! Ma chluinneas tu
ni uime cuir fios do'm ionnsuidh gun dail. Cha
chluinnear ach connsachadh agus caineadh anns a'
chomunn sin. Tha mi toilichte a chluinntinn gum
bheil sibh a' cumail gu math agus an teaghlach mar
an ceudna. Bha sinn fo amharus uimpe. Chluinneadh
sibh iomadh sgeul neonach aig comaidh nan seolad-
airean. Chuala an croitear gun robh an t-uachdaran
air ti a chur as a shealbh. Bha na gillean an impis
dol fodha an uair a rainig am bata gus an (or, g'an)
tearnadh. Co bhuaidh a chuala tu an sgeul sin?
Chroch iad a' mharag m'a (mu a) mhuineal. Is caraid

dhomh-sa an duine uasal mu'n do labhair e anns an
oraid a thug e seachad an raoir. Co mu'm bheil thu
a' gearan? Ciod mu'n robh sibh a' bruidhinn?
C'ainm dhuit? Iain Mac a'Ghobhainn, le ur cead.
Thog e lamh g'a bualadh. Chuir e gairdeachas oirnn
am faicinn cho sona. Bha an t-uisge a' dol an
doimhnead mar a b' fhaide a bha sinn a' dol a mach
air an loch. De rinn e leis a chuid leabhraichean?
Runaich e am fagail aig an taigh an aite an toirt air
falbh leis. Tamull an deidh sin, thill e g'an trusadh
ach bha a leabhraichean uile aon chuid caillte no
sgriosta.

Translation

I shall hear that story to-morrow. I beg your
pardon. I said that I would hear that story to-morrow.
Excuse me. I don't hear too well. Do you hear me,
Iain? I do, mother. Did you hear anything from
them since they went to America last year? I never
heard a word. Did anybody hear the like! If you
hear anything about him, send word to me without
delay. Nothing but argument and back-biting are
heard in that society. I am pleased to hear that you
are keeping well and the family likewise. We were in
(under) doubt about her. You would hear many a
queer story at the sailors' mess. The crofter heard
that the landlord was bent on putting him out of his
holding. The boys were on the point of going under
when the boat arrived to rescue them. From whom
did you hear that story? They hung the pudding
about his neck. The gentleman about whom he spoke
in the speech he made last night is a friend of mine.
Whom are you complaining about? What were you
speaking about? What is your name? John Smith,
sir. He lifted a hand to strike her. We rejoiced to
see them so happy. The water was getting deeper the
further we were going out on the loch. What did he
do with his books? He decided to leave them at
home instead of taking them away with him. A while
after that he returned to collect them but all his books
were either lost or destroyed.

LESSON 39

NA H-ABAIR ACH BEAGAN ACH ABAIR GU MATH E, Don't say much but say it well.

This old proverb is one of thousands in which the Gael embodies his philosophy of life. ABAIR! (**ab-ir**) say! The 'H' between the two 'A's' above makes for ease in pronunciation. Using ABAIR! we might say AN ABAIR SIBH FACAL RIS A' BHALACH? Will you say a word to the boy?

CHAN ABAIR MI SION (DAD) IDIR, I shall say nothing at all. SION (**she-un**) 1. particle, small amount.

CHAN ABAIREAR (or ABRAR) DAD TUILLIDH AIR A' CHUIS SIN, Nothing more will be said on that subject.

BAILE MOR RIS AN ABRAR INBHIR NIS, A large town called Inverness.

Now we have already found that some doing-words in Gaelic have two forms, a principal one, and a second one which is used after AN (AM), CHA, NACH, GUN (GUM), etc. This happens with the doing-word we are now considering. Now the principal form for ABAIR in future time is THEIR (**hayr**).

THEIR MI SIN RI SEUMAS ACH CHAN ABAIR MI RI PEADAIR E, I shall say that to James but I shall not say it to Peter. In the same way MA (GED) THEIR IAD NACH SOIRBHICH LEAT RO MHATH ANNS AN T-SUIDHEACHADH SIN, If (although) they say that you will not succeed very well in that situation. lit. it will not prosper with you. SOIRBHICH LE (**soruv-eeCH**) prosper with. There is no -EAS form and so we say MA (GED) THEIR.

THEIREAR AN CRUINNE NO AN CRUINNE-CE RIS AN T-SAOGHAL SEO, A CHIONN GUM BHEIL E CRUINN MAR PHEILEAR, This world is called the Globe or the Universe because it is round like a bullet (or, ball). lit. The Globe or the Universe is said to this world, etc. CRUINN **(krooing)** round. CRUINNE **(kroon-ya)** 1. globe. CRUINNE-CE **(kroonya-kay)** 1. universe. PEILEAR **(pay-lar)** 1. bullet (or ball).

THEIRINN MORAN NITHEAN ACH BITHIDH MI 'NAM THOSD, I could say many things but I shall be silent. TOSD **(tosd)** 1. silence. 'NAM THOSD, in my silence. THEIRINN **(hay-ring)** I should, could say.

NACH ABAIREADH TU GUN ROBH AN DUINE SIN AS A RIAN? Would you not say that that man was out of his mind? RIAN **(reean)** 1. order, method. AS A RIAN, out of his normal ways. ABAIREADH **(abir-uGH)** or ABRADH.

THEIRTEADH RIS MEALLTAIR ACH CHAN ABAIRTEADH RIS MEIRLEACH, He might be called a cheat but he couldn't be called a thief. MEALLTAIR **(myall-ter)** 1. cheat, imposter.

ABAIREAM **(abir-am)** let me say. ABAIR-EAMAID, let us say. ABAIREADH E, I, IAD, let him, her, them say.

ABAIREADH E MAR A THOGRAS E, Let him say as he pleases. TOGAIR! **(tOg-ir)** desire! incline!

The rest of this doing or saying-word you already know. THUIRT, also spelt THUBHAIRT **(hooirch)** said. AG RADH, saying: A RADH, to say.

There are three little words that we use in every other phrase in English. These are May, Can and Must, and these in Gaelic are FAOD **(food)**, URRAINN **(ooring)** and FEUM **(faym)**. As we have already dealt with URRAINN we shall now consider FAOD and FEUM. The following examples will make their use clear:

AM FAOD MI TIGHINN A STEACH? May I come in? FAODAIDH, Yes. NACH FAOD CAT SEALLTUINN AIR RIGH? May a cat not look at a king? CHAN FHAOD AN GILLE BEAG DOL A CHÒIR NAN EIREAGAN. The little boy mustn't go near the pullets. A CHOIR **(a cho-ir)** near to, in vicinity of, followed by 'of' form of name-word. EIREAG **(erag)** 2. pullet. CHAN FHAOD **(Chan**

ood) CHAN is used because FH is silent when sharpened by CHA and here it is followed by a vowel.

MUR FAOD MI FEOIL ITHEADH AM FAOD MI UIBHEAN NO IASG A GHABHAIL? If I may not eat flesh-meat may I take eggs or fish? DH'FHAODADH TU AN DA CHUID A GHABH-AIL ACH UIBHEAN AN ROGHAINN AIR IASG A CHIONN LUACH A' BHIDH A TH' ANNTA. You might take both but eggs in preference to fish on account of their food value. AN ROGHAINN AIR **(an roo-ing er)** In preference to (on). ROGH-AINN, 1. choice. ROGHNAICH! **(roo-neeCH)** choose! LUACH **(loo-aCH)** 1. value, worth.

AM FEUM THU FALBH CHO TRATH? FEUM-AIDH. MATA, MUR FHEUMADH, DH'FHAOD-ADH TU FUIREACH GUS AM FEASGAR LEINN. Must you go so early? I must. Well, if you didn't require to, you could have stayed till evening with us. DH'FHEUMADH E CEAD FHAOTAINN A CHUM IASGACH ANNS AN LOCH SIN. He had to get a permit to fish in that loch. A CHUM **(a Chum)** in order to. DH'FHEUMADH **(yaym-uGH)** required or would need.

DH'FHEUMADH SIBH A BHI CINNTEACH GUN TIGEADH E MU'N DO CHEANNAICH SIBH AITE-SUIDHE DHA ANNS AN TAIGH-CLUICHE. You would require to be certain that he could come before you bought a seat for him in the theatre. MU **(moo)** before. AITE-SUIDHE **(ach-a soo-ya)** 1. seat. TAIGH-CLUICHE **(ta-ee clooeeCH-a)** 1. theatre.

MA DH' FHEUMAS MI FALBH, FALBHAIDH MI. If I have got to go, I shall. DH'FHEUMTEADH SUIL GHEUR A CHUMAIL AIR. A sharp eye would require to be kept on him. DH'FHEUM-TEADH **(yaym-chuGH)** would require to be.

The two words ROIMH **(ro-ee)** before, and TROIMH **(tro-ee)** through, join up with MI, TU, etc., in exactly the same way.

ROMHAM **(ro-am)** before me. ROMHAD **(ro-ad)** before thee (or, you). ROIMHE **(roy-a)** before him, it. ROIMHPE **(roy-pa)** before her, it. ROMHAINN

(ro-ing) before us. ROMHAIBH **(ro-iv)** before you. ROMHPA **(ro-pa)** before them. Similarly, TROMHAM **(tro-am)** through me. TROMHAD, etc.

Faclair

SRUTHAIL! **(sroo-il)** rinse! BROCHAN **(bro-CHan)** 1. porridge. SMID **(smij)** 2. syllable. SUAIN! **(sooayn)** wind! wrap! STALL **(sta-ool)** 1. bandage. FIRINN **(feer-ing)** 2. truth. NEACH **(nyeCH)** 1. person, individual. EOLACH **(yolaCH)** acquainted. NA'S EOLAICHE **(nas yoleeCH-a)** more acquainted (followed by AIR). SOLAR **(solar)** 1. supply, provision. RIARACHAIL **(reeraCH-il)** satisfactory. CEARTAICH! **(kyarst-eeCH)** correct! CEART-ACHADH **(kyarstaCH-uGH)** correcting. BOGLACH **(bOg-laCH)** 2. marsh, quagmire. SLIGHE **(slee-ya)** 2. way. GU CLIS **(goo kleesh)** quickly. FIOR **(feer)** very (sharpens next word); also means true. GOIREASAN **(guras-an)** necessities, conveniences. LEABHAR-LATHA, 1. diary. DI-CHUIMHNEACH **(jeeCHoon-yaCH)** forgetful. CUIR ROIMHE, decide, determine. AN IAR **(an yeer)** western. CLAR, 1. plate. STAILINN **(stal-ing)** 2. steel. TORA, 1. drill, auger. IS GANN, 'tis scarcely.

Gaelic to English

Abair ri Mairi a' phoit a shruthladh. Feumaidh mi am brochan a bhruich a nis. Na h-abair smid. Bha Eilidh bheag ag radh gun do ghearr i a h-ordag leis an sgian. Shuain a mathair stall uimpe. Chan abradh e smid gus an d'fhosgail (or, an do dh' fhosgail) e an litir. Mur d'thuirt thu sin, co thuirt e ma ta? Abradh esan mar a thogras e, chan abair mise ach an fhirinn. Ma their sibhse rud, their esan a chaochladh. Theireamaid tuilleadh ach cha deanadh e a bheag de mhath. Chan abairinn uiread ri sin ris an neach ud gus am bithinn na's eolaiche air. Am faod mi dol a mach, a mhathair? Faodaidh, ma tha do leasanan air an deanamh. Mur 'eil, chan fhaod. Faodar a radh gum bheil daoine na's miosa na e anns a' bhaile. Chan fhaodar a radh gum bheil an solar-uisge anns a' bhaile seo ro riarachail. Dh' fhaodamaid ur faicinn

mu naoi uairean anns a' mhaduinn am maireach.
Dh' fhaoidteadh gum bheil do charaid tinn air neo
thigeadh e fada roimhe seo. Am feum sinn na
mearachdan anns an leabhar-chunntasan a cheart-
achadh a nis? Chan fheum. Bidh uine gu leoir againn
air son sin am maireach. Ma thuiteas tu anns a'
bhoglaich sin, feumaidh tu do shlighe a thoirt a mach
cho math agus a dh' fhaodas tu. Ma dh' fheumas
tu falbh gu clis, thoir leat do mhaileid bheag agus
fior-bheagan ghoireasan-turuis. Dh' fheumteadh
leabhar-latha a bhi agam leis cho di-chuimhneach
agus a tha mi. Tha feum aice air pailteas uisge teth
agus siabuinn air son na nigheadaireachd. Gabh
romhad. Ghabh iad romhpa. Chuir sinn romhainn
gun toireamaid sgriob do na h-Eileanan an Iar. Bha
na clair-stailinn cho cruaidh agus is gann a rachadh
an tora tromhpa.

Translation

Tell Mary to rinse the pot. I must boil the porridge
now. Mum's the word. Little Helen was saying that
she cut her thumb with the knife. Her mother wound
a bandage round it, i.e. bandaged it. He wouldn't say
a syllable until he had opened the letter. If you didn't
say that, who said it then? Let him say as he pleases.
I'll say (nothing) but the truth. If you say one thing
he'll say the opposite. We could say more but it
wouldn't do much good. I wouldn't say as much as
that to that person until I should be better acquainted
with him. May I go out, mother? You may, if you
have done your lessons. If not, no. It may be said
that there are worse folk than him in town. It can't
be said that the water supply in this town is very
satisfactory. We could see you to-morrow about nine
o'clock in the morning. Perhaps (it could have been
that) your friend is sick otherwise he would have
come long before now. Must we correct the mistakes
in the account book now? No, we shall have time
enough for that to-morrow. If you fall in that marsh
you must make (take) your way out as well as you
may (can). If you have to go off quickly, take with
you your little bag and very few travel necessities. I

would need to have a diary (with) so forgetful as I am. She needs plenty of hot water and soap for the washing. Go on. They went on (or, along, forward). We decided that we would pay a visit to the Western Isles. The steel plates were so hard that the drill could scarcely go through them.

LESSON 40

FROM time to time we have used numbers in our lessons, but now we shall make a closer study of them. Here they are: AON (**oon**) one. DHA (GHa) or DA, two. TRI (**tree**) three. CEITHIR (**kay-hir**) four. COIG (**kOig**) five. SE (**shay**) six ; also SIA (**sheea**). SEACHD (**sheCHk**) seven. OCHD (**oCHk**) eight. NAOI (**nooee**) nine. DEICH (**jayCH**) ten.

Now for the 'teens' which start from eleven. AON-DEUG (**oon-jayg**) eleven. DHA-DHEUG (**Gha-yayg**) twelve. TRI-DEUG (**tree-jayg**) thirteen. CEITHIR-DEUG (**kay-hir-jayg**) fourteen, and so on up to FICHEAD (**feeCHad**) twenty. Notice that we have said DHA-DHEUG and not DA DEUG. DA DHEUG is only used when the name-word is included, i.e., DA UAIR DHEUG. Twelve hours or times.

From twenty onwards we have AON AIR FHICHEAD (**oon ayr eeCHad**) twenty-one, lit. one on twenty. DHA AIR FHICHEAD (**GHa-ayr-eeCHad**) twenty-two, and so on to DEICH AIR FHICHEAD, thirty. AON-DEUG AIR FHICHEAD, thirty-one, lit. eleven on twenty. DHA-DHEUG AIR FHICHEAD, thirty-two. TRI-DEUG AIR FHICHEAD, thirty-three, etc., till we reach DA FHICHEAD (**da eeCHad**) forty, where we shall halt for the present. What we have learned we shall use to tell the time on the clock, UAIREADAIR (**oorad-ir**) Class 1. In passing note that after DA, two: FICHEAD, twenty: CEUD (**kayad**) hundred : MILE (**meela**) thousand, we use the same form of the name-word as for one person or thing. Thus DA, FICHEAD, COIG CEUD, TRI MILE EACH: Two, twenty, five hundred, three thousand horse(s). This often happens in English. AON and DA (or DHA) sharpen the first letter of the following word if possible. AON has no effect on D, T or S.

47

Let us begin with the hours. UAIR (**ooir**) 2. hour: UAIREAN (**ooir-an**) hours. UAIR (or, AON UAIR) one o'clock. DA UAIR, two o'clock. TRI UAIREAN, three o'clock. CEITHIR UAIREAN, four o'clock, and so on to DEICH UAIREAN, ten o'clock. For eleven, AON UAIR DEUG (**oonar-jayg**) and for twelve, DA UAIR DHEUG (**daoor-yayg**). In these last two the word for 'hour' has been put in the middle of the numbers.

LETH-UAIR (**lyay-ooir**) half-an-hour. CEATH-RAMH (**ker-ruv**) 1. quarter. CAIRTEAL (**karst-yal**) 1. quarter: this word is used chiefly in the north.

The minutes are: MIONAID (**meenij**) 2. a minute. DA MHIONAID, two minutes. TRI MIONAIDEAN, three minutes onwards to DEICH MIONAIDEAN, ten minutes. AON MHIONAID DEUG (**oon veenij jayg**) eleven minutes. DA MHIONAD DHEUG (**da veenij yayg**) twelve minutes, etc., to FICHEAD MIONAID, twenty minutes.

The over-twenties are: MIONAID AIR FHICHEAD (**meenij ayr eeCHad**) twenty-one minutes. DA MHIONAD AIR FHICHEAD, twenty-two minutes. TRI MIONAIDEAN AIR FHICHEAD, twenty-three minutes, and so on to DEICH MIONAIDEAN AIR FHICHEAD, thirty minutes, or LETH-UAIR, half-hour. Remembering how we did with the '-teens', we often find TRI MIONAIDEAN FICHEAD, twenty-three minutes. CEITHIR MIONAIDEAN FICHEAD, twenty-four minutes and so on.

For past the hour, we say AN DEIDH (**an jay**), and for to the hour, we say GU (**goo**).

DE'N UAIR A THA E? (**jayn ooir a ha eh**)—stress (**ooir**) What time is it? Here are some answers. THA E UAIR, It is one o'clock. THA E MIONAID AN DEIDH (GU) UAIR, It is a minute past (to) one. THA E DA MHIONAID AN DEIDH (GU) UAIR, It is two minutes past (to) one. THA E AON MHIONAID DEUG AN DEIDH (GU) DA UAIR, It is eleven minutes past (to) two. THA E FICHEAD MIONAID AN DEIDH (GU) TRI (UAIREAN), It is 20 minutes past (to) three. From three o'clock onwards to ten o'clock, the word UAIREAN may be omitted.

CEATHRAMH (or COIG MIONAIDEAN DEUG) AN DEIDH (GU) AON UAIR DEUG, A quarter past (to) eleven. LETH-UAIR AN DEIDH DA UAIR DHEUG, Half-past twelve. TRI MIONAIDEAN FICHEAD (or AIR FHICHEAD) AN DEIDH (GU) NAOI, Twenty-three minutes past (to) nine.

MEADHON-LA (**mayon la**) mid-day. MEADHON OIDHCHE, midnight.

Money is counted in much the same way. NOT (**not**) a pound sterling. NOTAICHEAN (**noteeCH-an**) pounds stg. PUNND (**poond**) 1. is usually a pound in weight though still used for money. PUINND (**pooend**) pounds. SGILLINN (**skeeling**) 2. penny: also used for pence. SGILLINNEAN (**skeeleen-yan**) pennies.

CIA MEUD? (**ka mayd,** stress **mayd**) how much? how many? followed by form or name-word as for one person or thing, e.g. CIA MEUD EACH? How many horses? CIA MEUD DUINE? How many persons? CIA MEUD A THA SEO? How much is this? DE 'PHRIS A THA AN LEABHAR? What is the price of the book? A' PHRIS (**a freesh**) 2. the price. DE 'PHRIS A THA NA STOCAINNEAN? What's the price of the stockings? DA FHICHEAD SGILLINN, forty pence. DE 'PHRIS A THA AN DEISE? What is the price of the suit? COIG NOTAICHEAN DEUG, fifteen pounds

For size or distance the words are: MEUDACHD (**mayd-aCHk**) 2. size, magnitude ; also MEUD (**mayd**) 1. size, greatness. AIRDEAD (**ar-jad**) 2. height, or AIRDE (**ar-ja**) 2. height. LEUD (**layad**) 1. breadth. FAIDEAD (**fa-jad**) 2. or, FAIDE (**fa-ja**) 2. length. DOIMHNEAD (**don-yad**) 2. or DOIMHNE (**don-ya**) 2. depth. MILE (**meela**) 2. mile. SLAT, 2. yard. TROIGH (**tro-ee**) 2. foot ; also the sole of the foot. OIRLEACH (**or-lyach**) 2. inch. AITHEAMH (**ae-huv**) 2. fathom: AITHEAMHAN (**aee-yan**) fathoms.

Short forms AIRDE, FAIDE, DOIMHNE more usual.

DE'N MHEUDACHD A THA ANNS AN TOGAIL SIN? What is the size of that building? TOGAIL (**tOkil**) 2. building. THA E TRI TROIDHEAN DEUG AIR AIRDE, OCHD TROIDHEAN DEUG

AIR FAIDE AGUS DA THROIDH DHEUG AIR LEUD, It is thirteen feet in (on) height, eighteen feet in length and twelve feet in breadth (or width).

DE'N T-ASTAR A THA EADAR AN DA BHAILE? What is the distance between the two towns? COIG MILE DEUG, fifteen mile(s).

DE'N FHAIDE A THA ANNS AN AODACH? What length is in the cloth? SEACHD SLATAN DEUG, DA THROIGH AGUS NAOI OIRLICH GU LETH, seventeen yards, two feet and nine and a half inches. GU LETH (goo lyay) and a half.

DE'N DOIMHNEAD A THA ANNS AN LOCH? What depth is the loch? SEACHD AITHEAMHAN, seven fathoms ; or THA E SEACHD AITHEAMHAN AIR DOIMHNEAD, It is seven fathoms in depth.

DE'N CUDTHROM A THA ANNS A' CHLOICH SIN? What weight is in that stone? SE TUNNACHAN DEUG, sixteen tons: or THA I SE TUNNACHAN DEUG AIR CUDTHROM, It is sixteen tons in (on) weight. CUDTHROM (koodrum) 1. weight. TUNNA, 1. ton. CEUD-CHUDTHROM (kayad CHoodrum) 1. hundredweight. PUNND (poond) 1. pound (money or weight). UNNSA (oonsa) 1. ounce: UNNSACHAN, ounces. CLACH, 2. stone.

Note that LA, day and BLIADHNA, year, when followed by DEUG use the form of the name-word as for one thing. COIG LA DEUG, a fortnight: lit. fifteen days. SEACHD BLIADHNA DEUG, seventeen years.

How high, long, broad, etc., is translated by DE CHO ARD'S, DE CHO FAD'S, DE CHO LEATHANN'S, etc. DE CHO ARD'S A THA AN TAIGH SIN? How high is that house? DE CHO LEATHANN'S A THA AN ABHAINN? How broad is the river? LEATHAN (lyay-an) broad. DOMHAIN (do-in) deep.

Faclair

A CHUID A'S MO, the majority, most. FAIRGE (farug-a) 2. sea. A STIGH (a staaee) inside (no motion). A MUIGH (a mooee) outside (no motion). AM FEAR, each. AN TE, each for Cl. 2. words. MUTHADH (moo-uGH) 1. change. SEACHD SGITH,

thoroughly tired (of). MIOS (**mee-us**) 1. month. AIR
THOISEACH (**er hosh-uCH**) in advance, fast. AIR
DHEIREADH (**er yayr-uGH**) behind. TOMHAIS!
(**to-ish**) measure! i.e. weigh, survey, guess. TOMHAS
(**to-as**) 1. measure, or weight. TOILICH! (**tol-eeCH**)
please! UIRSGEUL (**oor-skayl**) 1. novel, romance.
PAISG! (**pashg**) wrap! PASGADH, wrapping.
EILEAN MHANAIN (**aylan vannin**) Isle of Man.
CAITH! (**ka**) spend! wear! CAITHTEACH
(**ka-chaCH**) lavish, prodigal. CAOMHAINN! (**koov-
ing**) save! spare! economise! CAOMHNADH
(**koov-nuGH**) economising, or economy, Class 1.
COTHROMAICH! (**korum-eeCH**) weigh! MEIDH
(**mayee**) 2. a balance; also weigh! POCAN
(**poCHkan**) 1. bag, poke. COTHROM (**korum**)
1. a weight. MEALLTAIR (**myaool-ter**) 1. cheat.
SLIGE (**sleega**) 2. scale, pan of balance, shell.
NA'S MO, either, nor. SOMHAIRLE (**so-ar-lya**)
Samuel. COMHDHAIL (**ko-el**) 2. meeting. COMH-
DHAIL MHATH ORT, good meeting on you, used
by second person to the one leaving him. AOIS
(**ooish**) 2. age. ULAIDH (**ool-ee**) 2. treasure.
UGHDAR (**oo-dar**) 1. author. DE NA? what? DE
NA THA DE? how much? FEAR, 1. TE, 2. One
person or thing.

Gaelic to English

De'n uair a tha e? Seachd mionaidean fichead (or
air fhichead) gu ochd. Coig uairean feasgar. Cia meud
iasg a ghlac sibh? Da fhichead. Gasda. Ghlac mi a'
chuid a's mo dhiubh ann an uair an uaireadair. De'n
doimhne a tha anns an fhairge taobh a muigh an
eilein? Mu choig aitheamhan deug air fhichead. Cia
meud a thug sibh air a' chota sin? Seachd notaichean
deug. Nach e a bha daor? Cha robh. Bha e gu
math saor agus bha mi gle thoilichte a fhaotainn.
De pris nam peann-luaidhe? Coig sgillin an t-aon.
Thoir dhomh fear, ma's e do thoil e. Tapadh leat.
De na tha agad de dh' airgiod? Tha deich sgillin.
C'uin a thainig e dhachaidh? Rainig e Di-mairt mu
leth-uair an deidh uair anns a' mhaduinn. Bha e seachd
sgith de'n turus, an duine bochd. De'n aois a tha thu a

bhalaich? Tha mi aon bhliadhna deug agus ochd miosan. De cho ard's a tha thu? Coig troighean, ceithir agus tri-ceathramhan oirlich. Nach d' thug thu fainear gun robh d' uaireadair da mhionaid dheug air thoiseach. Tha thu cearr. Tha e tri mionaidean deug air dheireadh. De faid' an aodaich a tha anns a' chorn sin? Fan gus am faigh mi an t-slat-thomhais. Tha direach naoi slata(n) deug, aon troigh agus seachd oirlich gu leth ann. 'S e sin ri radh, troigh agus ceithir oirlich gu leth goirid air fichead slat. Innis dhomh de rinn thu air (or, an deidh) duit dol a steach do'n bhuth. Mata, cheannaich mi leabhar a thoilich rium gu mor, uirsgeul a chaidh sgriobhadh le ughdar Albannach. Is e 'Eilean na h-Ulaidhe' ainm an leabhair. An deidh do fhear a' bhutha an leabhar a phasgadh, chuir mi not air a' bhord agus fhuair mi fichead sgillin air ais. Mar a chi sibh, thug mi ceithir-fichead sgillinn air an leabhar. De cho fada 's a bha sibh ann an Eilean Mhanain? Coig la deug. Chaith mi cuid mhor de m' airgiod ann. B' fhearr dhomh a bhi air a chaomhnadh an aite bhi cho caithteach. Cothromaich am pocan siucair seo dhomh, a Shomhairle, ma's e do thoil e. Cuir air a' mheidh e mata. Am bheil na cothroman ceart? Tha fhios gum bheil. Shaoileadh tu gur mealltair a th' annam. Chan 'eil dad cearr air a' mheidh na's mo. Tha e coig unnsachan a dhith air da phunnd. Gun robh math agad. 'S e do bheatha. Slan leat, a Shomhairle. Comhdhail mhath ort, a Sheumais.

Translation

What time is it? Twenty-seven minutes to eight. Five p.m. How many fish did you catch? Forty. Fine. I caught the most of them in the space of an hour. What depth is the sea outside of the island? About thirty-five fathoms. How much did you give for that coat? Seventeen pounds. Wasn't it dear? It was not. It was fairly cheap and I was very pleased to get it. What's the price of the pencils? Fivepence each. Give me one if you please. Thank you. How much money have you? Ten pence. When did he come home? He arrived (on) Tuesday about half-past one in the morning. He was thoroughly sick of the journey, the poor chap. What age are you, my lad? I am eleven years and eight months. How tall are you? Five feet, four and three-quarter inches. Didn't you notice that your watch was twelve minutes fast? You are wrong. It is thirteen minutes slow. What length of cloth is in that bale? Wait and I'll get the measuring rod. It is exactly nineteen yards, one foot, seven and a half inches. That is to say, one foot, four inches and a half short of (on) twenty yards. Tell me what you did after going into the shop. Well, I bought a book that pleased me greatly, a novel that was written by a Scots author. Treasure Island is the name of the book. After the shop-keeper wrapped up the book, I laid a pound on the counter and I got twenty pence back. As you see, I paid (gave) eighty pence for the book. How long were you in the Isle of Man? A fortnight. I spent a lot of my money there. I would have been the better of saving it instead of being so lavish. Weigh this bag of sugar for me if you please, Samuel. Put it on the balance then. Are the weights just? Of course they are. You would think I am a cheat? There is nothing wrong with the balance either. It is five ounces short of (of want on) two pound. Thank you. You're welcome. Bye, bye, Samuel. Good-bye, James.

LESSON 41

THE Gaels count in scores, or to a base of twenty as the mathematicians would say, and a native speaker could without hesitation render ' Ninety-three ' by TRI-DEUG AGUS (or 'S) CEITHIR FICHEAD, i.e. Thirteen and four twenties: or in a second way, CEITHIR FICHEAD AGUS A TRI-DEUG, i.e. Four twenties and thirteen. This second way is perhaps the easier for the learner. Traces of this method of counting are still to be found in French, and when shepherds reckon their sheep by scores.

Before any number up to twenty it is customary to put an A- (or A H- if a vowel follows) unless a name-word is mentioned. For instance, in answer to the question CIA MEUD BRADAN A GHLAC THU? How many salmon did you catch? I might answer GHLAC MI TRI, CEITHIR, COIG, etc., BRADAIN ; I caught three, four, five, etc., salmon: or, GHLAC MI A TRI, A CEITHIR, A COIG, A H-OCHD, A COIG-DEUG, A FICHEAD, A TRI-DEUG AIR FHICHEAD, etc. I caught three, four, five, eight, fifteen, twenty, thirty-three. Two would be, A DHA (**a GHa**) ; and twelve, A DHA-DHEUG.

Now let us consider the numbers. 40, DA FHICHEAD (**da eeCHad**). 41, DA FHICHEAD 'S A H-AON or AON 'S DA FHICHEAD. DA FHICHEAD BATA 'S A H-AON, forty-one boats: or we might say, AON 'S DA FHICHEAD BATA, always remembering that after FICHEAD, twenty, CEUD, hundred, MILE, thousand, MUILLEAN (**mool-yan**) 1. million, the form of the name-word used is the same as that for one single person or thing. Continuing our series we reach 50. DEICH AIR DA FHICHEAD, or DA FHICHEAD 'S A DEICH, or, more shortly, LETH-CHEUD (**lyay-CHeead**). 51 men, LETH-CHEUD

54

FEAR 'S A H-AON, or AON FHEAR DEUG AGUS DA FHICHEAD, or DA FHICHEAD FEAR 'S A H-AON-DEUG. 53. TRI FIR DHEUG 'S DA FHICHEAD, or DA FHICHEAD FEAR 'S A TRI-DEUG, or LETH-CHEUD FEAR 'S A TRI. The TRI FIR DHEUG should be noticed. Just as we say FIR MHORA, and not FIR MORA, the I of FIR (men) causing the M to be sharpened, so also is DEUG sharpened after FIR and such others, e.g., CEITHIR BUILG DHEUG, fourteen bags. BALG (**balug**) 1. bag. BUILG (**booilug**) bags.

This happens with name-words whose form for more than one person or thing has an I as its last vowel. So SEACHD EICH DHEUG, seventeen horses, but SEACHD TAIGHEAN DEUG, seventeen houses.

99 men: CEITHIR FICHEAD FEAR 'S A NAOI-DEUG, or NAOI-DEUG 'S CEITHIR FICHEAD FEAR. 100 men: CEUD FEAR. 101 men: CEUD FEAR AGUS A H-AON. We could also have said for these last two examples, COIG FICHEAD FEAR, 100 men; and COIG FICHEAD FEAR AGUS A H-AON, 101 men. 129 men: CEUD 'S NAOI AIR FHICHEAD FEAR, or SE FICHEAD FEAR AGUS A NAOI. 150 men: CEUD GU LETH FEAR or SEACHD FICHEAD FEAR 'S A DEICH. GU LETH (**goo lyay**) and a half more, which in this case is fifty. MILE GU LETH, 1500. Be careful, however, with the small numbers; e.g. TRI OIRLICH GU LETH. Three and a half inches, not Three inches and a half of three extra.

198 horses: CEUD AGUS CEITHIR FICHEAD EACH 'S A H-OCHD-DEUG, or NAOI FICHEAD EACH 'S A H-OCHD-DEUG. 200 horses: DA CHEUD EACH or DEICH FICHEAD EACH. After 200 it is better to use CEUDAN, hundreds.

793 horses: SEACHD CEUD AGUS CEITHIR FICHEAD EACH 'S A TRI-DEUG. CEUD is sharpened by AON, DA, TRI, CEITHIR, but not by COIG upwards.

5,479 yards: COIG MILE AGUS CEITHIR CHEUD. TRI FICHEAD SLAT 'S A NAOI-DEUG. AGUS and 'S can be varied or often left out. We

55

could also have said COIG MILE, CEITHIR CHEUD, NAOI-DEUG 'S TRI FICHEAD SLAT.

7,382,539 of a population: SEACHD MUILLEAN, TRI CHEUD AGUS CEITHIR FICHEAD MILE 'S A DHA, COIG CEUD 'S NAOI-DEUG AIR FHICHEAD SLUAIGH. SLUAGH (**sloo-aGH**) 1. population, people, public.

The use of DA is a little bit different and so we have left it to the last. As before, note it is used instead of DHA with name-words and sharpens the name-word and any describing-word which follows. DA CHAT MHOR, two big cats. DA BHEATHA SHONA, two happy lives. Again, DA always takes the form of the name-word as for one person or thing after it, i.e. Two cat, life, horse, tree, etc., just as we say in English, Two ton.

Now, if you will refer to Lesson 24 where we dealt with the changes which took place in Name-words after words such as Of, on, with, on, etc., you will understand what follows more readily. Take the word CRAOBH, tree, Class 2. BARR NA CRAOIBHE, the top of the tree. BARR NA CRAOIBHE MOIRE, the top of the big tree. AIR A' CHRAOIBH MHOIR, on the big tree. Now note this last example and put in DA instead of AIR A' and you have DA CHRAOIBH MHOIR, two big trees. Now put in DHEUG instead of MHOIR and you have DA CHRAOIBH DHEUG, twelve trees. Similarly with CLACH, 2. stone. DA CHLOICH MHOIR, two big stones. DA CHIRC BHAIN, two white hens. DA CHIRC BHAIN DHEUG, twelve white hens. But CUDTHROM AN DA CHLOICHE MOIRE, the weight of the two big stones.

The little word Gu (**goo**) means To, towards, up to. It can also mean, In order to. Now GU joins with MI, TU, etc., in the same way as LE, AIR, etc., but seems to get a bit changed in the process. Thus CHUGAM (**hoogam**) to me. CHUGAD (**hoogad**) to thee. CHUIGE (**hooig-a**) to him or it. CHUICE (**hooiCH-ka**) to her (or it). CHUGAINN (**hoog-ing**) to us. CHUGAIBH (**hoog-iv**) to you, CHUCA (**huCH-ka**) to them.

CHUIR E LITIR CHUGAM ACH CHA DO CHUIR
MI FIOS-FREAGAIRT CHUIGE FHATHAST. He
sent me a letter, but I haven't sent him an answer yet.
CHUIGE IS UAITHE, to and fro.

CHUN (**CHoon**), also written CHUM, has likewise
the meaning of to, towards. CHOISICH E CHUN
AN DORUIS. He walked to(wards) the door ; and it
is used in this sense instead of DO. It takes the 'of'
form the name-word after it.

Faclair

CIA LION? (**ka leen**) how many? BLIADHNA-
LEUM (**bleea-na-laym**) 2. leap year. BARRACHD
(**bar-raCHk**) 2. surplus, superiority, also used for
'more', 'extra'. BEINN NIBHEIS (**nyiv-ish**) Ben Nevis.
BEINN NAM FAOGHLA (**foo-la**) Benbecula. AIR
A' CHUID AS LUGHA (**er a CHooj as looa**) at least.
GILLE-LITREACH (**leech-raCH**) postman ; also,
POSTA. MOTHACHADH (**mo-aCH-uGH**) 1. consciousness, feeling. SORAIDH (**so-ree**) 2. compliments,
best wishes, farewell. CARN-SLAOID (**slooeej**) 1.
sledge. CLO (**klo**) 1. homespun cloth. DE NA THA?
How much is? ADHAR (**aGH-ar**) 1. air. ASTAR, 1.
distance, space, journey.

Gaelic to English

Cia meud each a tha a' ruith an diugh? Da fhichead
's a coig. Cia lion cathair a tha anns an talla? Tha
ochd fichead 's a tri-deug. Tha anns an sgoil seo
ceithir cheud agus seachd 's tri fichead balach (also,
tri fichead 's a seachd balaich) agus coig ceud, naoi
agus da fhichead caileag. Tha mile agus se-deug de
sgoilearan ann uile gu leir. Cia meud sgillinn a tha
ann an not? Tha ceud. Tha tri cheud, tri fichead
's a coig de laithean anns a' bhliadhna agus la a
(or de) bharrachd anns a' bhliadhna-leum. De'n
airde (or airdead) a tha ann am Beinn Nibheis?
Ceithir mile, ceithir cheud troigh agus a se. De
cho fada 's a tha e eadar Glaschu agus Beinn
nam Faoghla a' dol troimh an adhar? Mu cheud gu
leth mile 's a h-ochd de dh' astar. De na tha de

chlo air (a) fhagail? Cha do thomhais mi fhathast e,
ach tha mi a' deanamh dheth gum bi air a' chuid as
lugha tri fichead slat ann. De a' bhliadhna a tha (an)
seo? Naoi ceud deug, leth cheud 's a ceithir. Chaidh
e chun an doruis a dh' fhaicinn an robh an gille-
litreach a' tighinn. Sgriobh iad litir chugaibh. Chaill
e a mhothachadh agus thainig e chuige fhein tri
uairean a dh' uine an deidh sin. Tha e gu falbh anns
a' mhaduinn. Bha sinn deas gu falbh an uair a thainig
an t-uisge. Thoir mo shoraidh g' ur brathair. Thoir
chugam na tha air fhagail de'n fhiodh agus ni sinn
carn-slaoid do'n ghille bheag.

Translation

How many horses are running to-day? Forty-five.
How many chairs are in the hall? One hundred and
seventy-three. There are in this school four hundred
and sixty-seven boys and five hundred and forty-nine
girls. There are one thousand and sixteen scholars
altogether. How many pence are in a pound?
A hundred. There are three hundred and sixty-
five days in the year and one (of) extra in the
Leap-year. What height is (in) Ben Nevis? Four
thousand, four hundred and six feet. How far is it
between Glasgow and Benbecula going by (through)
the air? About one hundred and fifty-eight miles of a
journey (or, distance). How much homespun cloth is
left? I haven't measured it yet, but I suppose that
there will be at the least sixty yards in it. What year
is this (here)? Nineteen fifty-four. He went to the
door to see if the postman was coming. They wrote a
letter to you. He lost consciousness and came to
(himself) three hours (of time) afterwards. He is to go
off in the morning. We were about to go away when
the rain came. Give my compliments to your brother.
Bring me what's left of the wood and we will make a
sledge for the little boy.

LESSON 42

IN this lesson we shall try to put the numbers we have lately learned into serial order, e.g., first, second, third, etc. We shall take them along with the word LA, day.

AN CEUD LA, the first day. Often this is written A' CHEUD (a CHeeud) both for Class 1 and 2 name-words. A' CHEUD BHORD, the first table. A' CHEUD BHROG, the first shoe. CEUD is also used for one hundred as we saw in the last lesson. AN DARA LA, the second day. AN TREAS LA (tress) the third day. AN CEATHRAMH LA (ker-uv) the fourth day. AN COIGEAMH LA (kOeeg-uv) the fifth day. AN SEATHAMH LA (shay-uv) the sixth day. AN SEACHDAMH LA (sheCHk-uv) the seventh day. AN T-OCHDAMH LA (oCHk-uv) the eighth day. AN OCHDAMH CRAOBH, the eighth tree. AN NAOIDHEAMH LA (nooee-uv) the ninth day. AN DEICHEAMH LA (jayCH-uv) the tenth day. Of the above numbers CEUD alone sharpens the name-word which follows.

With the 'teens' it is to be noted that after Class 2 words all the DEUG's are sharpened to DHEUG; and, again, we use AONA (oona) for First, instead of CEUD. AONA sharpens a Class 2 word.

AN T-AONA LA DEUG, the eleventh day. AN AONA CHRAOBH DHEUG, the eleventh tree. This means, The first day, tree, with ten added on. AN DARA LA DEUG, the twelfth day. AN DARA CRAOBH DHEUG, the twelfth tree. AN TREAS LA DEUG, the thirteenth day. AN TREAS CRAOBH DHEUG, the thirteenth tree, and so on to AM FICHEADAMH LA (feeCHad-uv) LA, the twentieth day; but AN FHICHEADAMH CRAOBH (an yeeCHad-uv) the twentieth tree. AN T-AONA LA FICHEAD, the twenty-first day, i.e., the first day, with twenty added. AN AONA CHRAOBH

59

FICHEAD, the twenty-first tree. AN DARA LA FICHEAD, the twenty-second day. AN DEICH-EAMH LA FICHEAD, the thirtieth day.

AN T-AONA LA DEUG AIR FHICHEAD, the thirty-first day. AN AONA CHRAOBH DHEUG AIR FHICHEAD, the thirty-first tree, the eleventh tree on twenty. AN DARA LA DEUG AIR FHICHEAD, the thirty-second day. AN DARA CRAOBH DHEUG AIR FHICHEAD, the thirty-second tree, and so on to AN DA FHICHEADAMH LA (CRAOBH), the fortieth day (tree). AN DA FHICHEADAMH LA 'S A H-AON, the forty-first day: or AN T-AON 'S AN DA FHICHEADAMH LA, i.e., The fortieth day and one, or, The one and fortieth day.

AN DA FHICHEADAMH LA 'S A DHA, or, AN DA 'S AN DA FHICHEADAMH LA, the forty-second day, and so on to AN DEICH 'S AN DA FHICHEADAMH LA, the fiftieth day: or AN DA FHICHEADAMH LA 'S A DEICH: or again AN LETH-CHEUDAMH LA (lyayCHad-uv). There is more than one way of rendering the numbers in Gaelic, but the method of casting out the scores and throwing the remainder to the end is the easiest.

The fifty-first day would thus be AN DA FHICHEADAMH LA 'S A H-AON-DEUG, but you can also hear said AN LETH-CHEUDAMH LA 'S A H-AON, or AN T-AONA LA DEUG THAR DA FHICHEAD, the eleventh day over forty. AN CEITHIR FICHEADAMH LA, the eightieth day. AN CEITHIR FICHEADAMH LA 'S A H-OCHD-DEUG, the ninety-eighth day. AN CEUDAMH LA, or AN COIG FICHEADAMH LA, the hundredth day.

The 119th day is AN CEUDAMH LA 'S A NAOI-DEUG, or AN NAOIDHEAMH LA DEUG THAR A' CHEUD, or AN COIG FICHEADAMH LA 'S A NAOI-DEUG. THAR A' CHEUD, over the hundred. THAR (har) over, across, followed by 'of' form of name-word. AN CEUD AGUS AN COIG-DEUG 'S TRI FICHEADAMH LA, the one hundred and seventy-fifth day, or more simply AN CEUD AGUS

AN TRI FICHEADAMH LA 'S A COIG-DEUG.
AN DA CHEUDAMH LA, the two hundredth day.
AN SEACHD CEUD AGUS AN CEITHIR
FICHEADAMH LA 'S A NAOI-DEUG, the seven
hundred and ninety-ninth day. AM MILEAMH LA,
the thousandth day. MILEAMH (meel-yuv). AN
TRI-DEUG AIR DA FHICHEAD MILE, SE CEUD
AGUS DA FHICHEADAMH FEAR 'S A H-OCHD-
DEUG, the 53,658th man. AM MUILLEANAMH
FEAR, the millionth man.

AM MIOSACHAN

We call a calendar in Gaelic MIOSACHAN (mees-
aCHan) 1. The months of the year are AM FAOIL-
TEACH (fool-tyaCH) 1. January. AN GEARRAN
(gyarran) 1. February. AM MART (marst) 1. March.
AN GIBLEAN (geeb-lan) 1. April. AN CEITEAN
(kay-chan) 1. May. AN T-OG-MHIOS (an tog veess,
accent on tog) 1. June. AN T-IUCHAR (an chooCHur)
1. July. AN LUNASDAL (loonas-dal) 2. August.
AN SULTUINE (soolt-in-ya) 1. September. AN
DAMHAIR (dav-ir) 2. October. AN T-SAMHUINN
(an tav-ing, accent on tav) 2. November. AN
DUDLACHD (dood-laCHk) 2. December.

LAITHEAN NA SEACHDUINE
Days of the Week

DI-DOMHNUICH (jee doneeCH) 1. Sunday ; also
LA NA SABAID (sabij) 1. Sabbath day. DI-LUAIN
(looayn) 1. Monday. DI MAIRT (marsht) 1. Tuesday.
DI-CEUDAOIN (keead-un) 1. Wednesday. DIAR-
DAOIN (jeear-dooeen, accent on doo) 1. Thursday.
DI-H-AOINE (hooin-a) 1. Friday. DI-SATHUIRN
(sa-hurn) 1. Saturday. SEACHDUIN (sheCH-doon) 2.
week.

NA RAIDHEAN

The seasons or RAIDHEAN (raee-an) from RAIDH,
2. quarter (of a year) are: AN T-EARRACH (char-
raCH) 1. Spring ; AN SAMHRADH (savruGH, or
saoo-ruGH) 1. Summer ; AM FOGHAR (fo-ar) 1.
Autumn ; AN GEAMHRADH (gev-ruGH, or gayoo-
ruGH) 1. Winter.

Faclair

A BHEAG, any, the least. THAIRIS AIR, over,
across. FAICHE (**faee-CHa**) 2. sports (or drill)
ground. COMH-AINM (**kO enum**) 1. anniversary.
LA BREITH (**la bray**) 1. birth-day. ATH (**a**) next,
following. CEANN-TEAGAISG (**kyann chekishk**) 1.
text. RANN (**raoon**) 2. verse, division. RUGADH
(**rook-uGH**) was born. CAOCHAIL! (**kooCH-il**)
change! die! BLAR, 1. field, plain. ALLT NA
BANAIG, Bannockburn. MU DHEIREADH (**moo
yay-ruGH**) last. OIDHCHE SHAMHNA (**oyCHa
haoo-na**) 2. Hallowe'en. A REIR (**a rayr**) according
to. SOISGEUL (**sosh-kayl**) 1. gospel. A LOS, in
order to. CAIBIDEIL (**kepij-il**) 1. chapter.

Gaelic to English

Tha ceithir raidhean anns a' bhliadhna. Is e
Di-domhnuich a' cheud la de'n t-seachduin agus Di-
Sathuirn an seachdamh. Tha an Nollaig a' tuiteam
air a' choigeamh la fichead de'n Dudlachd. Bha an
t-Earrach gle fhuar am bliadhna agus cha robh an
Samhradh a bheag na b' fhearr. Leugh am Ministear
an t-seachdamh salm deug thairis air an t-se fichead.
Chaidh gach ficheadamh craobh anns a' choille a
ghearradh sios an t-seachduin seo chaidh. Thainig an
sluagh nan ceudan do'n fhaiche feasgar Di-mairt a los
na farpuisean fhaicinn. Bhris air a shlainte anns an
ochdamh bliadhna dheug de a aois. Is ann air an la
mu dheireadh de'n Lunasdal a gheibh mi mo laithean
saoire. Chi mi thu seachduin bho'n diugh: 's e sin ri
radh, air an t-seathamh la fichead de'n mhios seo.
Tha seachduin an de o'n dh' fhalbh e. Their sinn an
Sultuine ri dara mios an Fhoghair agus an t-Samhuinn
ri ceud mios a' Gheamhraidh. Is e an diugh, an
ceathramh la fichead de'n Cheitean, comh-ainm la-
breith Ban-righ Bhictoria. Their sinn Oidhche
Shamhna ris an aona la deug air fhichead de'n
Damhair, agus an t-Samhuinn ris an ath-mhios.
Gheibh sibh an ceann teasgaisg anns an t-Soisgeul a
reir Eoin, an coigeamh caibideil deug agus an treas
rann deug. Rugadh Raibert Burns air a' choigeamh

62

la fichead de'n Fhaoilteach anns a' bhliadhna seachd
ceud deug, da fhichead 's a naoi-deug agus chaochail
e air an aona la fichead de'n Iuchar anns a' bhliadhna
seachd ceud deug ceithir fichead 's a se-deug. Chaidh
Blar Allt na Banaig a chur air a' cheathramh la
fichead de'n Og-mhios anns a' bhliadhna tri ceud
deug agus ceithir deug.

Translation

There are four seasons in the year. Sunday is the
first day of the week and Saturday the seventh.
Christmas falls on the twenty-fifth day of December.
Spring was very cold this year and Summer was not
any better. The minister read the one hundred and
thirty-seventh psalm. Every twentieth tree in the wood
was cut down this last week. The public came in their
hundreds to the playing-field on Tuesday evening to
see the contests. His health broke (lit. broke on his
health) in the eighteenth year of his age. It's on the
last day of August that I shall get my holidays. I shall
see you this day week: that is to say, on the twenty-
sixth day of this month. It is a week yesterday since
he went away. We call the second month of Autumn
September and the first month of Winter November.
To-day, the twenty-fourth of May, is the anniversary
of the birthday of Queen Victoria. We call the thirty-
first day of October, Hallowe'en, and the next month,
November. You will find the text in the Gospel
according to John, the fifteenth chapter and the
thirteenth verse. Robert Burns was born on the
twenty-fifth of January, 1759, and died on the twenty-
first of July, 1796. The battle of Bannockburn was
fought on the twenty-fourth day of June, 1314.

LESSON 43

THE boxing of the compass is a sailor's accomplishment, but for those who spend their lives on land a few directions will suffice. The compass is called AN IUL-CHAIRT (**yool-CHarsht**) 2. or IUL-CHAIRT A' MHARAICHE, The mariner's compass. MARAICHE (**mar-eeCHa**) 1. a mariner. The points or directions are AIRDEAN (**ar-jan**) from AIRD (**arj**) 2. airt, direction.

In taking his bearings, the Gael faced AN EAR ('**nyerr**), East or towards the rising sun. Behind him was AN IAR ('**nyeer**) West. IAR is an old word meaning after or behind. To his right was DEAS (**jayss**) the South. DEASAIL or DEISEAL (**jaysh-al**) southward (or lucky). To his left was TUATH (**tooa**) the North. TUATHAL (**tooa-hal**) to the left, contrary to the course of the sun (hence wrong or unlucky). SHEOL E TUATH AGUS DEAS, AN EAR AGUS AN IAR. He sailed north and south, east and west.

Often we find AIRD used along with these points. THAINIG NA DRUIDHEAN O'N AIRD AN EAR GU IERUSALEM, The wise men came from the east to Jerusalem. DRUIDH (**drooee**) 1. Druid, wise man.

THA GAOTH NA H-AIRDE TUATH (or, A' GHAOTH TUATH) GLE FHUAR, The north wind is very cold.

THA SINN A' STIURADH A TUATH, A DEAS. We are steering north, south. 'A' is often put in before DEAS and TUATH. STIUIR! (**styu-ir**) steer!

BHA E A' FUIREACH AN CEANN A TUATH AN EILEIN. He was staying in the north end of the island. BHA A BHRATHAIR AIR AN TAOBH AN EAR. His brother was on the east side.

Westward and Eastward are occasionally translated by SIAR (**sheear**) and SEAR (**sherr**). CHAIDH AM BATA FODHA LETH-CHEUD MILE SIAR AIR

64

BARRAIDH, The boat sank (went under) fifty miles westward of Barra. BARRAIDH **(barr-aee)** Barra. We could also have said AIR TAOBH AN IAR BHARRAIDH.

Other directions are AN EAR-THUATH **('nyerr(a) hooa)** North-East. AN IAR-THUATH **('nyeer(a) hooa)** North-West. AN EAR-DHEAS **('nyerr(a) yayss)** South-East. AN IAR-DHEAS **('nyeer(a) yayss)** South-West.

CHAIDH IAD CHUM (or GUS) AN IAR-DHEAS AN SAMHRADH SEO CHAIDH, They went to the South-West last summer. Lit. This summer (that) went.

There are two more action-words which do not form their past time according to the rule we have given in a previous lesson. Of these the first is BEIR! **(bayr)** meaning Bear! bring forth! or when followed by AIR, on meaning Bear on! overtake! catch! The past-time is RUG **(roog)**. Here are some examples.

RUG A' CHAORA UAN, The sheep bore (gave birth to) a lamb.

RUG IAD AIR AN AISEAG, They caught the ferry. AISEAG **(ashug)** 1. ferry.

RUG E AIR LAIMH ORM, He caught me by the hand. lit. He bore on hand on me.

CHA B' FHADA GUS AN ROBH SINN A' BREITH ORRA, It was not long till we were overtaking them. BREITH **(bray)** overtaking: to overtake, A BHREITH.

BHA IAD A' BREITH AIR A CHEILE, They were catching each other.

BEIRIDH I MAC, She shall bear a son. The rest of the action-word BEIR is quite regular. Do not, however, mix up BHEIRINN. I should give, with BHEIRINN, I should bear, and likewise BHEIR-EADH, which can mean either 'would bear' or 'would give' in both cases. BHEIRINN DUAIS DHUIT NAM BEIREADH TU AIR A' CHU SIN DHOMH. I would give you a reward if you would catch that dog for me.

RUIG! **(rooeeg)** means Reach! arrive! extend! and its past-time is RAINIG **(raneeg)** reached, etc., and also RUIG **(rooeeg)** in many places.

RAINIG E AN TAIGH FLIUCH AGUS SGITH, He reached (or arrived) home wet and tired.

DE'N UAIR ANNS A' MHADUINN A RUIGEAS TU LUNNAINN? What time in the morning will you reach London? RUIGIDH MI MU OCHD UAIREAN. I shall arrive about eight o'clock.

THOIR A NUAS AN DEALBH BHARR A' BHALLA, Take the picture down off the wall. CHAN URRAINN DOMH RUIGSINN AIR, I can't reach it. RUIGSINN (**rook-shing**) reaching or extending, attaining. AIR, on, when used with RUIG and its various parts shows effort towards, e.g., BU MHIANN LEIS A BHI BEARTACH, He would like to be rich. CHA RUIG E AIR SIN, He will never attain that. A NUAS (**a nooas**) from above. THIG A NUAS, come down (from above). THIG A NIOS (**a nyees**) come up (from below).

Used with LEAS (**layss**) 1. profit, advantage, we have CHA RUIG E A LEAS AN SGEUL SIN INNSE DHOMH. He needn't tell me that story: he will not reach (his) advantage, betterment, he won't improve matters, he needn't.

CHA DO RUIG (RAINIG seldom used here) IAD LEAS A BHI CHO SGAITEACH, They needn't have been so sarcastic. SGAITEACH (**skach-aCH**) sharp-tongued.

How often do we hear the words: He very nearly, or almost did, or came within a little of doing such and such a thing. The little word THEAB (**hayb**) translates this. THEAB MI TUITEAM, I almost fell. TUITEAM (**tooch-am**) falling. THEAB NACH DO CHUIREADH E AN SAS, It was a near thing that he was not taken into custody (arrested). SAS 1. custody. AN SAS AN, Engaged in doing something.

With TUIT! fall! in its various parts we have phrases such as AN COMHAIR A CHINN, in the direction of his head, headlong. AN COMHAIR A CHUIL, In the direction of his back, backwards. AN COMHAIR A BHEOIL, In the direction of his mouth, forwards. BEUL, mouth. CUL (**kool**) 1. back.

THUIT E AN COMHAIR A CHINN, He fell head-long. COMHAIR (**ko-ir**) 2. direction.

Faclair

CEANN-UIDHE (**kyann-ooee**) 1. destination. FIOS-RAICH? (**feess-reeCH**) enquire! FIOSRACHADH (**feess-raCH-uGH**) enquiry, enquiring. FEAR-CUIRN (**fer-coorn**) 1. outlaw. FEAR-TATHAICH (**fer-ta-eeCH**) 1. visitor. SIUBHAIL! (**shoo-el**) go away! walk! die! ARSA, said, quoth. MU THUATH, in the north, north. MU DHEAS, in the south, south. TAIGH-COMHNUIDH (**co-nee**) 1. dwelling-house. SNAMHAICHE (**snaveeCH-a**) 1. swimmer. TIUG-AINN! (**choo-ging**) come along! TROBHAD (**trO-ad**) SEO! Come hither! THUGAD! (**hoogad**) Take care! SIUTHAD! (**shooad**) proceed! AS MO LETH, on my behalf. BODHAIR! (**bo-er**) deafen! BODHRADH (**bo-ruGH**) deafening. SABAID (**sab-ij**) 2. row. DEASBUD (**jaysbud**) 1. debate, discussion. FIMI-RIDH (or, FEUMAIDH) must. GU H-ARD, up high.

Groups of persons from two to ten are: DITHIS (**jeeish**) two, a couple. TRIUIR (**trooir**) trio, three. CEATHRAR (**kayrar**) quartette, four. COIGNEAR (**kOig-nyur**) quintette, five. SEANAR (**shaynar**) sextette, six. SEACHDNAR (**sheCHk-nar**) seven. OCHDNAR (**ochK-nar**) eight. NAOINEAR (**nooeen-ar**) nine. DEICHNAR (**jayCH-nar**) ten.

CIA MEUD A BH'ANN? BHA OCHDNAR, How many were there? Eight.

Gaelic to English

Rainig iad dhachaidh anns an fheasgar. Cha ruig thu an t-Oban a' dol an rathad sin. C'uin' a ruigeas sibh ur ceann-uidhe? Chan 'eil fhios agam, agus cha ruig thu leas tuilleadh fhiosrachadh. An ruigear a leas am bord a charachadh? An do ruig e a leas sin a dheanamh? Ruig air an ord a Sheumais. Cha d' rainig na balaich air na h-ubhlan a bha gu h-ard air a' chraoibh. Beir orm ma's urrainn thu. Beiribh air a' mheirleach! Thuirt am fear-cuirn nach beireadh na saighdearan air beo. Rug iad air a' mheirleach mu'n d' fhuair e as. Rug i mac do'n righ ach shiubhail i air an dara la an deidh a bhreith. Am bheil na cearcan a' breith an drasda? Tha, rug iad fichead ubh

an diugh ach is ann anns an Earrach is pailte a
bheireas iad. Chaidh an duine a bhreith gu bron.
Rug i air laimh air. Bheirinn duais duit nam beireadh
tu air a' chu sin dhomh. Am bheil sibh a' dol an iar
an diugh? ars' an t-osdair ris an fhear-tathaich. Chan
'eil, fhreagair esan, ach tha mi a' dol an iar-thuath.
Co as a tha e? As Alba mu thuath? Chan ann, as
Alba mu dheas. Is ann an taobh an ear a'bhaile is
bitheanta a gheibhear na taighean-comhnuidh as sine.
Theab mi breith air. Theab i a cas a bhriseadh an
uair a thuit i leis a' chreig. Nach do theabadh a
bhathadh an de? Cha do theabadh. Tha e 'na
shnamhaiche laidir. Tiugainn leam do Mhuile am
bliadhna. Trobhad seo, a Mhairi, agus dean eisdeachd
ri do mhathair. Thugad! Tha car a' tighinn. Siuthad!
tha pailteas air a' bhord. Thuit an t-ard-shagart an
comhair a chuil agus chaidh a mharbhadh. Rinn e sud
uile as mo leth. Ni sibh mo bhodhradh le ur sabaid.
Cha dean mi do chiurradh. Rinn e am milleadh. Cia
meud duine a bha anns a' chuideachd? Bha deichnear
ach dh fhalbh dithis dhiubh mu'n robh an deasbud
seachad. Falbh a nunn agus fan thall gus an abair
mi riut tighinn a nall. Fimiridh mi feitheamh ris a'
phosta. Thig crioch air a h-uile rud. Slan leibh!

Translation

They reached home in the evening. You won't reach
Oban going that way. When will you reach your
destination! I don't know and you needn't enquire
further. Does the table need to be moved? Did he
need to do that? Reach for the hammer, James. The
boys could not reach the apples that were high up on
the tree. Catch me if you can. Catch the thief! The
outlaw said that the soldiers would never catch him
alive. They caught the thief before he got away. She
bore a son to the king, but she died on the second day
after his birth. Are the hens laying at present? Yes,
they laid twenty eggs to-day but it is in the spring
that they lay most plentifully. (The) man was made
(born) to mourn. She caught him by the hand. I would
give you a reward if you would catch that dog for
me. Are you going west to-day? said the innkeeper

to the visitor. No, he replied, but I am going north-west. Where is he from? From the north of Scotland? No, from the south of Scotland. It is in the east end of the town that most often are found the oldest dwelling-houses. I almost caught him. She came within a little of breaking her leg when she fell over the rock. Was he not almost drowned yesterday? No. He is a strong swimmer. Come along with me to Mull this year. Come here, Mary, and listen to your mother. Look out! a car is coming. Go ahead. There is plenty on the table. The high priest fell backwards and was killed. He did all that on my behalf. You will deafen me with your fighting. I won't hurt you. He spoilt them. How many persons were in the company? Ten, but two of them left before the discussion was over. Go over and stay over till I say to you to come over. I must wait for the postman. All things come to an end. Good-bye.

VOCABULARY

A

Ab (aba, abachan) 1. abbot.
Abair (radh) say.
A bheag, very few or little ; hardly any.
A chaochladh, its opposite.
A cheart, the very, just.
A choir, near to, in vicinity of. It is followed by 'of' form of name-word.
A chuid, his or its share (of).
A' chuid is mo (de), the greater part of, the majority.
A chum, in order to.
A dha, two. Use Da before name-word.
Adhar (adhair) 1. air, atmosphere ; also Athar.
A dhith, wanting or lacking.
A dh' ionnsuidh, towards, to.
Aghaidh (aghaidh, aghaidhean) 2. face.
Agus, and : also 'as' in comparisons.
Air a' chuid a's lugha, at least.
Air culaobh, at back of, behind.
Aird (airde, airdean) 2. point of the compass or cardinal point.
Airde, 2. height. A dol an airde, getting higher.
Air dheireadh, behind ; slow, with regard to a watch or clock.
Air thoiseach, in front ; fast, with regard to a watch or clock.
Air ti, bent on, determined to.
Air uairibh, occasionally.
Aire, 2. notice, attention.
Aisig (aiseag), restore, ferry over.
Aite-suidhe (aiteachan-suidhe) 1. seat.
Aithisg (aithisge, aithisgean) 2. report.
A leth-taobh, to one side.
Allt na Banaig, 1. Bannockburn.

A los, in order to.
Am falach, in hiding, hidden.
Am measg, among, in midst (of).
Aitheamh (aitheimh, aitheamhan) 1. fathom.
Amharus (amharuis) 1. suspicion, doubt.
A muigh, out, outside ; but A mach means motion towards the outside.
An aghaidh, against (followed by 'of' form of name-word).
An aite, in place (of).
A nall, over, from the other side.
A nunn, over, to the other side.
An ceann, at the end or expiration (of).
An comhair, in direction (of).
An deidh, after.
An Ear, the East. An Ear-thuath, North-East. An Ear-dheas, South-East.
An Iar, the West. An Iar-thuath, North-West. An Iar-dheas, South-West.
A nios, from below.
An impis, almost, on the point of.
An lathair, in presence (of), present.
A nuas, from above.
Anmoch, late.
An t-Suain, Sweden.
Aon chuid . . . no, either . . . or
Aodann (aodainn, aodainnean) 2. face, visage. As an aodann, to the face, outright.
A riamh, ever.
Arbhar (arbhair) 1. corn.
Arsa, said, quoth.
As an aghaidh, outright, to the face.
As leth, to account (of). As mo leth, to my account, to my charge, also on my behalf.
A steach, into (implying motion).

A stigh, inside (implying rest there).
Ath, next again. An ath-uair, the next time.

B

Baile-fearainn, 1. farm.
Baillidh (baillidh, baillidhean) 1. bailiff.
Balg (builg, builg) 1. bag, wallet.
Ball (buill, buill) 1. member, ball.
Banas-taighe, 2. housewifery.
Barrachd, 2. superiority, overplus. Barrachd agus, more than.
Barraidh, Barra.
Beinn nam faoghla, Benbecula.
Beinn Nibheis, Ben Nevis.
Beir (breith), bring forth, produce, catch.
Beir air, catch up on, overtake.
Biadh (bidh, biadhan) 1. meat, food.
Biadh (biadhadh) feed, maintain.
Blar (blair, blair or blaran) 1. field ; also battlefield.
Blasda, tasty.
Bliadhna-leum, 2. leap-year.
Bochd, poor. Is bochd, 'tis a pity.
Bodhair (bodhradh), deafen.
Boglach (boglaich, boglaichean) 2. quagmire, swamp.
Bonn (buinn, buinn) 1. sole of foot.
Braigh-ghill, 1. pre-eminence.
Bras, swift, impetuous.
Brat-urlair, 1. carpet.
Breab (breabadh) kick.
Brochan (brochain) 1. porridge.
Buailteach (ri), liable or subject to.
Buannachd (buannachd) 2. gain, profit.
Buil (buil) 2. consequence, application, use.
Buin (buntainn) belong to, related to.

C

Caillte, lost.
Cain (caineadh) traduce, dispraise.
C'ainm? What name?

Caibideil (caibidil, caibideilean) 1. chapter.
Cairdeil, friendly.
Cairich (caradh), place, repair; also spelt Caraich, with first 'a' long.
Cairteal (cairteil, cairtealan) 1. quarter.
Caith (caitheamh or caitheadh) spend, wear, consume.
Caithteach, lavish, prodigal.
Cam, crooked, blind of an eye.
Caochail (caochladh) change, alter, die.
Caochladh (caochlaidh, caochlaidhean) 1. change, variety, difference, opposite.
Caoilte, Caoilte.
Caomhain (caomhnadh) spare.
Caomhnadh (caomhnaidh) 1. economy, saving.
Car (cuir, cuir) 1. twist, bend, trick.
Car (cair, caran) 1. car.
Caraich (carachadh) move, stir, The first 'a' is short.
Carn-slaoid, 1. sledge.
Casaid (casaide, casaidean) 2. complaint.
Cead, 1. leave, permission.
Ceannard (ceannaird, ceannardan) 1. chief, commander.
Ceann-teasgaisg (cinn-theagaisg, cinn-theagaisg) 1. text.
Ceann-uidhe (cinn-uidhe, cinn-uidhe) 1. destination.
Cearn (cearna, cearnan) 2. region, corner, kitchen.
Ceartaich (ceartachadh) correct, adjust, rectify.
Ceathramh (ceathraimh, ceathramhan) 1. quarter.
Ceathramh, fourth.
Ceathrar, four, quartette (persons).
Ceilear (ceileir) 1. warbling of birds.
Ceitean (ceitein) 1. month of May.
Ceithir, four.
Ceud, hundred.
Ceud-chudthrom or Ceud chothrom. 1. hundredweight.

Chun, to, towards, for.
Cia lion? How many?
Cia meud? How much? how many?
Ciall (ceille) 2. reason, sense, meaning.
Cisean (cisein, ciseanan) 1. hamper.
Ciuin, calm, gentle.
Cladach (cladaich, cladaichean) 1. stony beach.
Clar (clair, clair or claran) 1. plate, lid, deck of ship.
Clisgeadh (clisgidh, clisgidhean) 1. start, alarm. An clisgeadh, instantly.
Cliu 1. fame, praise, reputation.
Clo (clotha, cloithean) 1. home-spun cloth.
Coig-la-deug, fortnight.
Coignear, five, quintette (persons).
Comaidh (comaidh, comaidhean) 2. mess, eating together.
Comh-ainm (an la) 1. anniversary.
Comhair, 2. direction.
Comhdail mhath ort! Good luck to you! Comhdhail, 2. meeting.
Comhnard, level, equal, smooth.
Comhnard (comhnaird, comhnardan) 1. plain, field.
Comhnuich (comhnuidh) dwell, inhabit.
Comhnuidh (comhnuidhe, comhnuidhean) 2. dwelling, house. An comhnuidh, always, continually.
Connsachadh (connsachaidh) 1. contention, argument.
Cor (coir or cuir) 1. condition, state.
Cosnadh (cosnaidh) 1. employment, a job.
Cothrom (cothruim, cothroman) 1. weight, a weight, opportunity; fair-play.
Cothromach, just, fair, upright; honest.
Cothromaich (cothromachadh) weigh, make the same size.
Crann (croinn, croinn) 1. mast.
Crion, withered.

Croch (crochadh) hang.
Cruinne, 1. roundness, globe, the world, but Na Cruinne, of the world.
Cruinne-ce, 2. the world, the universe.
Cuan Mor, 1. Atlantic.
Cuaran (cuarain, cuarain) 1. slipper, sandal.
Cudthrom (cudthruim) 1. weight, heaviness.
Cudthromach, heavy, important.
Cuid (codach, codaichean) 2. share, property.
Cuideachd, 1. company.
Cuir roimhe, resolve.
Cum (cumail) keep, hold.
Cum a mach, maintain, insist.
Cunntas (cunntais, cunntasan) 1. account.
Currac (curraic, curraicean) 1. woman's head-dress.

D

Dail (dalach, dalaichean) 2. delay; also credit or trust.
Dail (dalach, dailthean) 2. riverside meadow.
Damhair, 2. October.
Dana, bold, presumptuous.
Dara, second.
Deagh, good (placed before the name-word).
Deanadach, diligent.
Deas, ready, finished; also south.
Deasaich (deasachadh) make ready, prepare, bake.
Deasbud (deasbuid, deasbudan) 1. discussion, dispute.
De b' aill leat (leibh)? What was your will? I beg pardon.
Deidh, after.
Deidh (deidhe, deidhean) 2. wish, propensity.
Deichnear, ten (persons).
Deireadh (deiridh, deiridhean) 1. end, conclusion.
Deiseil, ready; also southward. Deiseal is another spelling of word.

Deoch-laidir, 2. strong drink.
Deoch-slainte, 2. a toast.
Dh'fhaoidte, perhaps.
Di-chuimhneach, forgetful.
Di-luain, 1. Monday.
Di-mairt, 1. Tuesday.
Di-ciadaoin, 1. Wednesday.
Diardaoin, 1. Thursday.
Di-haoine, 1. Friday.
Di-Sathuirn, 1. Saturday.
Di-domhnuich, 1. Sunday; also La na Sabaide, Sabbath.
Dion (dionadh) protect.
Dion (diona) 1. shelter.
Dithis, two, a pair (persons).
Doimhne or Doimhnead, 2. depth. A' dol an doimhne, getting deeper.
Doire (doire, doireachan) 2. grove.
Domhail, dense, bulky.
Dorra, more difficult.
Droch, bad (used before the name-word).
Druidh (druidh, druidhean) 1. Druid.
Dudlachd, 2. December.
Duine sam bith, anyone at all.

E

Eagar (eagair, eagairean) 1. order, class, arrangement.
Ear, East. An taobh an Ear, the east side.
Earrach (Earraich), 1. Spring.
Eilean Mhanain, Isle of Man.
Eire, 2. Ireland.
Eireag (eireige, eireagan) 2. pullet.
Eolas (eolais) 1. knowledge.

F

Fa chomhair, opposite to, in anticipation of.
Faiche (faiche, faichean) 2. sports or drill-ground.
Faide, 2. length.
Faigh (faotainn, faighinn) get.
Failte (failte, failtean) 2. welcome.
Fainear, under consideration or notice.

Fairge (fairge, fairgeachan) 2. sea.
Famhair (famhair, famhairean) 1. giant.
Fann, faint, languid.
Faoilteach (faoiltich) 1. January.
Fasa, easier.
Fear aithisg, 1. reporter.
Fear cuirn, 1. outlaw.
Fear eagair, 1. editor.
Fear seolaidh, 1. director.
Fear tathaich, 1. visitor.
Fear turuis, 1. traveller. Fir (or Luchd) turuis, travellers, tourists.
Fearann (fearainn) 1. land, estate.
Fearchar, Farquhar.
Feairrd, better of.
Feum (feuma, feumannan) 1. need, use.
Feumaidh mi, I must, need to.
Feumail, needful, useful.
Fiach (fiachainn) try, see, show, taste; also Feuch.
Fiadhaich, wild, fierce.
Fichead, twenty. Ficheadan, twenties.
Fimiridh mi, I must.
Fionnar, cool, fresh.
Fion-dearg, 1. port wine.
Fior, true, genuine, very, i.e. Fior bhochd, very poor.
Fiosraich (fiosrachadh) enquire, ascertain.
Firinn, 2. truth.
Fodha, under, below.
Foghar (foghair) 1. harvest, autumn.
Freagarrach, suitable, responsible.
Fuasgladh (fuasglaidh, fuasglaidhean) 1. solution, relief, untying.
Furan (furain) 1. hospitality, welcome.
Furasda, easy.

G

Gabh air, beat, punish ; also pretend.
Gabh oran, sing a song.
Gabh mo leisgeul, excuse me.
Gabh romhad, go forward or along.

Gairdeachas (gairdeachais) 1. joy, rejoicing.

Geamhradh (geamhraidh, geamhraidhean) 1. winter.

Geannair (geannair, geannairean) 1. small hammer.

Gearain (gearan) complain.

Gearran, 1. February.

Giblean, 1. April.

Gille litreach, 1. postman.

Gin, 2. anyone.

Giorra, shorter. Giorrad, 1. shortness.

Giorraid, shorter of or for.

Giullachd, 2. management.

Gobha (gobhainn, goibhnean) 1. blacksmith.

Goid (goid), steal.

Goirid as, short distance off.

Goireasan-turuis, 1. travel necessities.

Greidheadh (greidhidh, greidhidhean) 1. thrashing; also toasting, curing.

Gu brath tuillidh, evermore.

Gu clis, quickly, smartly.

Gu h-ard, high up.

Gu leth, one half more.

Gu math dheth, well-off.

Gun robh math agad (agaibh) thank you.

Gus, until, to.

Guth (gutha, guthan) 1. voice, mention, report.

I

Iar, west. Iar-thuath, north-west. Iar-dheas, south-west.

Imich (imeachd) depart.

Ionnsaich (ionnsachadh) learn, teach, educate.

Is gann, 'tis scarcely.

Is leir dhomh, I can see.

Iuchair (iuchrach, iuchraichean) 2. key.

Iuchar (iuchair) 1. July.

Iul-chairt (iul-chairte, iul-chairtean) 2. mariner's compass.

L

Labhair (labhairt) speak. Labhair romhad, say on.

La breith, 1. birth-day.

Laidir, strong.

Laogh (laoigh, laoigh or laoghan) 1. calf.

Larach (laraich, laraichean) 2. site of a building, ruin.

Lasadan (lasadain, lasadain) 1. match.

La saor, 1. holiday. Laithean saora, holidays.

Lathair (lathaire) 2. presence. An lathair, present.

Leabhar-sgriobhaidh, 1. writing-copy. Leabhar-latha, 1. diary.

Leag (leagail or leagadh) knock down, lay down, fell.

Lean (leantuinn) follow, continue. Lean ris, stick to it.

Leanabh (leinibh, leanabhan) 1. child, infant.

Leas, 1. benefit, advantage, interest.

Leathann, broad.

Leir, 1. sight, power of seeing. Cha leir dhomh e, I cannot see it.

Leithid (leithide, leithidean) 2. like, fellow.

Leth-cheud, fifty.

Leth-uair, half-hour.

Le ur cead, by your leave, sir.

Luach, 1. value, worth.

Luaidh (luaidhe) 1. or 2. lead. Cothrom luaidhe, a weight of lead.

Luath, fast, swift.

Luath (luath) 2. ashes.

Luchairt (luchairte, luchairtean) 2. palace.

Luchd, people, folk. It is used instead of Fir when reference may be to women as well as men. Luchd-eisdeachd, hearers.

Luchd-tathaich, visitors.

Lugha, less.

Lunasdal (lunasdail) 2. August.

M

Maileid (maileide, maileidean) 2. bag, wallet.
Mair (mairsinn) last, live.
Mar, as, in same way.
Marag (maraig, maragan) 2. blood-pudding.
Maraiche (maraiche, maraichean) 1. sailor.
Mar an ceudna, likewise.
Margadh (margaidh, margaidhean) 1. market, sale.
Mar is fhaide, the further.
Mar sin leat (leibh) the same with you: said in reply to a salutation.
Mart (mairt) 1. March.
Ma ta, truly, indeed, well.
Meadhon-la, mid-day.
Mealltair (mealltair, mealltairean) 1. cheat, swindler.
Meas (measadh), consider, esteem, calculate.
Measg (measgadh) mix, mingle. Measg an te, mask the tea.
Measg (am measg) among, amidst.
Meidh (meidh, meidhean) 2. a balance for weighing.
Meidhich (meidheachadh) weigh; also Cothromaich.
Meud, 1. greatness, amount, size. A mheud 's, as many as. Meud an taighe, the size of the house.
Meudachd, 2. size, bulk, dimension.
Mile (mile, miltean) 2. mile.
Mile, thousand. Miltean, thousands.
Milseag (milseig, milseagan) 2. a sweet.
Mi-mhodhail, impolite, bad mannered.
Mionaid (mionaide, mionaidean) 2. minute.
Mios (miosa, miosan) 1. month.
Miosa, worse.
Miosachan (miosachain, miosachain) 1. calendar, monthly magazine.
Misde, the worse of.

Mnathan, women.
Mochthrath, 2. morning, dawn.
Motha, larger, greater; also Mo.
Mothachadh (mothachaidh) 1. sense of feeling, consciousness.
Mothaich (mothachadh) notice, perceive.
Mu dheas, south. Mu thuath, north.
Mu dheireadh, last, at last.
Muillean, million.
Muineal (muineil, muinealan) 1. neck of a person.
Mu'n cuairt, around.
Mur b'e, had it not been, were it not for.
Muthadh (muthaidh) 1. change, alteration. Change of money.
Mu thimchioll, around, concerning.

N

Naoinear, nine, nine persons.
Na's mo, either. Chan 'eil esan ceart na's mo, he isn't right eithir.
Neach, 1. person. Neach-eigin, someone. Neach no neach-eigin, someone or other.
Neo-bhlasda, insipid, tasteless.
Neo-chiontach, innocent.
Nochd (nochdadh) appear, disclose, show.
Not (notaichean) 1. note (sterling).

O

Ochd, eight.
Ochdnar, eight persons.
Og-mhios, 1. June.
Oidhche-Shamhna, 2. Hallowe'en.
Oirleach (oirlich, oirlich) 2. inch.
Olcas (olcais) 1. badness.
Oraid (oraide, oraidean) 2. speech.
Os cionn, above.

P

Paidh (paidheadh) pay.
Paisg (pasgadh) wrap up, fold up.
Peann luaidhe, 1. pencil. Peann-tan-luaidhe, pencils.

Peilear (peileir, peilearan) 1. bullet.
Pocan (pocain, pocain) 1. bag.
Pris (prise, prisean) 2. respect, price.
Punnd (puinnd, puinnd) 1. pound
in weight or money.

R

Raidh (raidhe, raidhean) 2. quarter
of a year, season.
Rann (rainn, rannan) 2. verse,
division.
Rannsaich (rannsachadh) search,
explore, examine.
Re, during.
Reidhlean (reidhlein, reidhleanan)
1. green, bowling green.
Reubalach (reubalaich, reubalaich)
1. rebel.
Rian (rian, rianan) 1. order, method.
Riarachadh (riarachaidh) 1. satis-
faction.
Riarachail, satisfactory.
Ri dheanamh, to be done.
Ro, very much, exceedingly.
Roghainn (roghainne, roghainnean)
2. choice, best of.
Roghnaich (roghnachadh) choose,
select.
Rug, bore (children or animals),
lay (egg). Rug e air, he caught
him.
Rugadh, was born.
Ruig, reach, arrive.
Ruisg (rusgadh), strip, peel.
Runaich (runachadh) decide,
resolve.

S

Sabaid (sabaide, sabaidean) 2. row,
brawl.
Samhradh (samhraidh, samhraidh-
ean) 1. summer.
Samhuinn (samhna) 2. November.
Saoghal (saoghail, saoghalan) 1.
world, lifetime.
Saoil (saoilsinn) think, imagine.

Sas (sais) 1. restraint, custody,
grappling with work. An sas an
rud-eigin, busy at something.
Se or sia, six.
Seachdnar, seven persons.
Seachduin (seachduine, seachduin-
ean) 2. week.
Seachd sgith, thoroughly tired or
disgusted.
Sealbh (seilbh, sealbhan) 1. posses-
sion, luck, fortune.
Seall (sealltainn) look, see, show.
Seanair (seanair, seanairean) 1.
grandfather.
Seanar, 1. six persons.
Sear, east.
Searbh, bitter, intolerable.
Seid (seideadh) blow.
Seoladh (seolaidh, seolaidhean) 1.
sailing, direction, address.
Sgailean-greine, 1. sunshade.
Sgaiteach, cutting, satirical.
Sgal (sgala, sgalan) 1. skirl of pipes,
blast.
Sgalag (sgalaig, sgalagan) 2. farm-
servant.
Sgilinn (sgilinne, sgillinnean) 2.
penny.
Sgreadan (sgreadain, sgreadain) 1.
shriek.
Sgriob (sgrioba, sgrioban) 2. visit,
excursion, furrow.
Sgriob (sgriobadh) scrape, scribble.
Sgriosta, destroyed.
Siar, west.
Sid (side) 2. weather.
Sine, older.
Sine, Jean.
Sion, 1. something, anything.
Sith (sithe, sithean) 2. peace, quiet-
ness.
Siubhail (siubhal) go, walk, die.
Siuthad, say away, go on, proceed.
Slainte, 2. health, toast.
Slat-thomhais, 2. measuring-rod,
ruler.
Slige (slige, sligean) 2. shell, scale
of a balance.
Slighe (slighe, slighean) 2. way,
path, road.

Sluagh (sluaigh, sloigh or sluaighean) 1. crowd, people, public.

Smeorach (smeoraiche, smeoraichean) 2. mavis, thrush.

Smid (smide, smidean) 2. syllable, word.

Smuain (smuaine, smuaintean) 2. thought.

Snamhaiche (snamhaiche, snamhaichean) 1. swimmer.

Snuadh (snuaidh) 1. hue, complexion.

Socrach, easy, comfortably, leisurely.

Soirbhich (soirbheachadh) prosper, succeed.

Soisgeul (soisgeil) 1. Gospel.

Solar (solair, solaran) 1. supply, provision.

Somhairle, Samuel.

Soraidh, 2. compliments, best respects, farewell.

Spairn (spairne) 2. effort, hard struggle.

Sruthail (sruthladh) rinse.

Stailinn, 2. steel.

Stall (staill, stallan) 1. bandage.

Stiuir (stiuradh) steer, guide.

Straighlich (straighliche) 2. rattle of traffic.

Stuadh (stuaidh, stuadhan) 2. billow, gable of house.

Suain (suaineadh) wrap round, entwine.

Suain (suaine) 2. deep sleep.

Suathan (suathain, suathain) 1. a rubber.

Sultuine, 1. September.

T

Tachair (tachairt) happen, meet with.

Taigh-cluiche, 1. play-house, theatre.

Taigh-comhnuidh, 1. dwelling-house.

Tamailt (tamailte, tamailtean) 2. disparagement, insult.

Tamull (tamuill, tamullan) 1. space of time.

Taobh a muigh, outside. Taobh a stigh, inside.

Tapadh leat (leibh) thank you.

Tapaidh, clever.

Tathaich (tathaich) visit often, frequent.

Teachd, 1. arrival, coming.

Teaghlach (teaghlaich, teaghlaichean) 1. family.

Tearn (tearnadh) save, escape; also spelt Tearuinn.

Teirinn (tearnadh) descend.

Teotha, hotter.

Tha fhios, there is knowledge, of course.

Thairis, over.

Thairis air, over, across, beyond.

Thar, over, across.

Theab, miss, have almost.

Thoir (toirt or tabhairt) give, take.

Thoir seachad, deliver, give order.

Thug, gave, brought.

Thugad ! out of the way! look to yourself.

Tighinn bhuaidh, get over it, i.e. illness, etc.

Timchioll, around, concerning.

Tiugainn, come let us go.

Togail (togalach, togalaichean) 2. building distilling.

Togair (togradh) please, desire eagerly. Ma thogair, it is a matter of complete indifference to me, who cares anyway!

Togarrach, cheerful, animated.

Toigh, agreeable. Is toigh leam, I like.

Toigheach, fond of, keen on.

Toileach, willing.

Toileachas-inntinn, 1. satisfaction, peace of mind.

Toilich (toileachadh) please, satisfy.

Toill (toilltinn) deserve, merit.

Tolman (tolmain, tolmain) 1. little mound, knoll.

Tomhais (tomhas) measure, guess.

Tomhas (tomhais, toimhsean) 1. measure, guess.

Tora (tora, toraichean) 1. auger.
Toradh (toraidh, toraidhean) 1. fruit, produce, consequence.
Tosd, 1. silence.
Treasa, stronger.
Treud (treuda, treudan) 1. flock, herd.
Triuir, three persons.
Troigh (troighe, troighean) 2. a foot.
Trobhad seo ! or Trothad seo! Come here!
Truimid, heavier for.
Trus (trusadh) gather up.
Trusgan (trusgain, trusgain) 1. clothes, dress.
Trusgan-samhraidh, summer-clothes.
Tuath, north. Tuathal, to the left, against the sun.
Tuigseach, sensible, intelligent.
Tum (tumadh) dip, immerse.
Tunna (tunna, tunnachan) 1. ton.

Turus (turuis, turusan) 1. or 2. journey, voyage.

U

Uachdar (uachdair, uachdaran) 1. top, surface.
Ughdar (ughdair, ughdairean) 1. author.
Uair (uaire uairean) 2. hour, weather.
Uaireadair, 1. watch, timekeeper.
Uair sam bith, anytime.
Ubhalghort (ubhalghoirt, ubhalghoirtean) 1. orchard.
Uidheam-turuis, 2. luggage.
Uiread, so much, as much.
Uirsgeul (uirsgeoil, uirsgeulan) 1. novel, romance.
Ulaidh (ulaidhe, ulaidhean) 2. treasure.
Ullachadh, 1. preparation.
Unnsa (unnsa, unnsachan) 1. ounce.

Printed by Martin's The Printers Ltd., Berwick upon Tweed